BJ Powell
Cambridge
1993

COLLECTED POEMS

CHRISTOPHER CAUDWELL
(Christopher St.John Sprigg)
Collected Poems
1924-1936

Edited and with an Introduction
by Alan Young

CARCANET

Acknowledgements

I am grateful to Rosemary Sprigg for her enthusiastic help in obtaining all the manuscripts of her brother's poetry, and for her informative reminiscences. My gratitude is due, too, to Paul Beard for his memories of Christopher and of the preparation of *Poems* (1939) which he edited with such care and sensitivity.

The Humanities Research Center, The University of Texas at Austin have been courteous and efficient as they always are.

Dr Alan Munton's bibliography of Christopher Caudwell in our *Seven Writers of the English Left: A Bibliography of Literature and Politics, 1916-1980* has been most valuable.

I wish to thank the British Academy for a grant awarded from the Small Grants Research Fund in the Humanities which helped me to complete this volume.

My thanks, too, to Rovena Townsend for her typing of much of the material at different stages of the project.

First published in 1986 by
Carcanet Press Ltd
208-212 Corn Exchange Buildings
Manchester M4 3BQ

All rights reserved

Copyright © Rosemary Sprigg 1986 (Text)
Copyright © Alan Young 1986 (Introduction)

British Library Cataloguing in Publication Data

Caudwell, Christopher
 Collected poems.
 I. Title
 821'.912   PR6037.P65

ISBN 0-85635-653-0

The Publisher acknowledges financial assistance from the Arts Council of Great Britain

Typeset by Bryan Williamson, Swinton, Berwickshire
Printed in England by SRP Ltd., Exeter

Contents

1. *EARLY POEMS (1924-1927)*

Sonnet on his 17th Birthday	29
Easter Thoughts from Summer	29
On 'A Public School Anthology'	30
Biographies	30
The Mound (Bradford 'Lays')	31
Translation of Catullus's 'Vivamus mea Lesbia'	32
Agnosis	32
On a Dead Cat	33
In the Aegean	33
On Dryden	33
from The Progress of Poetry (1)	34
from The Progress of Poetry (2)	34
Sick Bed	35
From the Greek (1)	36
From the Greek (2)	36
On a Novelist	36
The Stranger	37
May	37
The Recollection	37
The Captive	38
Autumnal	38
Circumstance	39
The Occasion	39
The Experience	40
November the Eleventh	40
The Recollection	40
The Confession	40
The Justified	41
The Salvation	41
God's Gospel	42
A Profession	43
The Uniform	44
The Conundrum	44
Consecration	45
The Dream	47
The Sign	48
The Assignation: 1916	49
The Firing Party: 1917	50

Smoke and Diamond   51
   The Pursuit   51
   Impregnable   51
   Reason   52
   The Double   52
   Predestination   53
   Ariel   53
   The Song of Songs   53
   The Chase   54
   Betrayal   54
   The Question   55
   The Answer   55
   The Physician   56
   The Road   56
   Courage   57
   The Dialogue   57
   Spring Thoughts   57
   The Search   58
   Matter   59
   Complexity   60
   The Device   60
   Smoke and Diamond   61
   More Proverbs   61

2. POINT OF DEPARTURE (poems 1928-1936)

Poet's Invocation   65
Polar Expedition   65
Poem: High on a Bough   69
The Dialectic: A Sestina   69
The Apostate   72
The Request   72
The Consolations of Religion   73
The Unspeakables   73
The Danger   75
The Weakness   75
The Nature of the Physical World   76
The Last Judgment   77
The Survival   78
The Tradition   79
To –   80
Classic Encounter   80

They Said	81
The Visitor	82
The Object	83
The Secret	84
The Audience	85
The Kingdom of Heaven	86
Agamemnon and the Poet	87
The Ecstasy	87
Five Translations from the Chinese	88
From the Greek Anthology	89
From the Same	89
On a Successful Publican	90
Thought, while gazing at Colonel X	90
On a Tory M.P.	90
In a Chart Room	90
Epigram	90
On a Barrister	91
On the Same	91
On an Employer of Native Child Labour	91
On a Wicked Man	91
Sales Pastoral	91
The Vigil of Venus	93
Kensington Rime	94
In Memoriam T.E. Shaw	98
Heil Baldwin!	99

3. *from POEMS (1939) (poems 1934-1936)*

Epitaph	119
The Hair	119
Hymn to Philosophy	121
Tierra del Fuego	121
Was It?	122
Donne's Reverie	123
The Stones of Ruskin	124
Classic Encounter	125
The Progress of Poetry	126
Essay on Freewill	127
The Coal	128
Twenty sonnets of Wm. Smith	129
The Art of Dying: An Elegy	137
Orestes	142

Introduction

Christopher Sprigg (Christopher Caudwell)* was killed in action in Spain early in 1937. He was twenty-nine years old. During the half-century which has elapsed since then only about a quarter of his poems have been published in full. This book prints nearly one hundred poems additional to the thirty-six included in the selection made by Paul Beard soon after Christopher's death (*Poems* [1939]). It now becomes possible for readers to assess Christopher Sprigg's poetic achievement fully for the first time, and, in making such an assessment, to appreciate his distinctive contribution to the literature of heroic action in our time.

Christopher Sprigg advocated poetry's power to change society for the better. To understand language and emotions fully, he believed, is also to understand how they are bound up with social institutions and relationships; the human thought and feeling which make poetry possible and valuable cannot function properly in a society which encourages individual citizens to create islands of selfhood. Christopher Sprigg's generosity of spirit has been remarked before:

> To read him is to become aware of a certain meanness in many contemporary critics, an unwillingness of the young critic to commit himself, not necessarily at all to Marxism or Communism, but to some large, noble, and generous enthusiasm for what human life at its best could be.

When he wrote this in the early 1950s in his book *The Modern Writer and his World*[1], G.S. Fraser was thinking mainly about Christopher Sprigg the man, as revealed in his prose studies – especially *Illusion and Reality, Studies in a Dying Culture, The Crisis in Physics*, and *Further Studies in a Dying Culture*. Perhaps the most important discovery from this much enlarged collection of his poems is how free from both self-absorbed neurosis and small-minded envy Christopher Sprigg was.

---

* Christopher Sprigg used several pseudonyms, but his real name has been used throughout this introduction. He introduced his mother's maiden name as one of his pseudonyms in 1936 (for his novel *This My Hand*). Paul Beard explains that Christopher Caudwell was a name "which he reserved for his serious work, saying that he was afraid of spoiling his reputation as a writer of thrillers. This reversal of the usual procedure was very characteristic of his reserve, and was a decision made with complete gravity". (*Poems* [1939], p.8).

The second son of Stanhope William Sprigg and Jessie Mary Sprigg (*nee* Caudwell), Christopher St. John Sprigg was born in Putney, London, on 20 October 1907. Like his elder brother, Theodore Stanhope Sprigg, Christopher was to be drawn inevitably into a family tradition of journalism and literary editing. His mother was a professional artist who died in 1916 at the age of 44. His father, born in Dublin in 1866, was the eldest son of a well-known newspaper editor, Captain Stanhope Sprigg, who edited the *Nottingham Guardian* and, later, *Berrows Worcester Journal*. Stanhope William Sprigg, who was educated at King's School, Worcester, followed his father into the profession of literary editor. He edited newspapers in Sheffield, Nottingham, and Southampton, and was founder-editor of the *Windsor Magazine* and of *Cassell's Magazine*. He became literary editor of the *Daily Express* and was New York representative of the *Standard*. During World War I he worked for the Ministry of Food as Assistant Director of the American section. After the war he acted as advisory editor to C. Arthur Pearson Ltd., and he founded a literary agency. He was the author of books about world affairs and he wrote several novels. In 1925 he married Grace Coxon, and a daughter, Rosemary, was born in 1929. He died in 1932.

Christopher Sprigg's childhood was spent in the village of East Hendred, at the eastern end of the Vale of White Horse. His father was a convert to Roman Catholicism and he sent his son to a Catholic college, Ealing Priory School (now St. Benet's). Here Christopher showed a relish and natural aptitude for disputation. His involvement in speculative philosophy, science, and poetry stem from his schooldays, too. One of his closest friends, Paul Beard – who edited the first selection of Christopher's poems – knew him at school. In his *Note* to the 1939 edition of the poems Beard recalled these enthusiasms:

> As a schoolboy, his interest both in poetry and in science was already well developed, but more noticeable at the time than either was his intellectual detachment, rather shocking to his schoolfellows, and the marked intellectual dexterity with which he would argue on behalf of views totally different from his own.

The earliest drafts of some of his poetry date from his final year at school, including the long sequence "November 11th" on which he worked intermittently between 1921 and 1926, and possibly later.

Christopher left Ealing Priory School before he was fifteen years old, his departure hastened by an incident involving a scrap of paper. Apparently, he refused to obey a prefect's order to pick up some litter because, Christopher claimed, he had not been responsible for dropping it. The main reason for the curtailment of his formal education, however, may have had less to do with his stubbornly determined stand against wrong authority (an inherited Sprigg family trait) and rather more to do with the family's temporary financial difficulties which ruled out the continuation of private education for Christopher. In November 1922, when he had just turned fifteen, he joined the staff of the *Yorkshire Observer* where his father was literary editor. In addition to training as a cub reporter covering local events, he also wrote unsigned reviews of novels for his father's literary pages.

Two years later he returned to London. In 1925, using the pseudonym St. John Lewis, he began to write for *Airways*, a monthly journal edited by his brother Theodore. Christopher's contributions included reviews of books and films as well as items of more general interest on the subject of flying. His topics sometimes included new technical developments in aviation ("Aerial wireless", for example) but it was the glamour of flight which drew most enthusiasm from him. "By Air to the Middle East", "Polar Exploration by Air", "Amundsen's Polar Flight", "A Night Flight to Paris", "The War in the Air", and "Aviation for Everyone" – such titles convey the range of this boyish romanticism. He continued to write for *Airways* (later *Air and Airways* and then *Airways and Airports*) until December 1933 when the journal was sold. In later reviews he sometimes used the pseudonym Christopher Beaumont but also signed many as C. St. John Sprigg or Christopher Sprigg. His enthusiasm for the world of flying was to continue unabated into five full-length works of popular journalism: *The Airship: Its Design, History, Operation and Future* (1931), *Fly With Me: An Elementary Textbook on the Art of Piloting* (1932) which he wrote with Captain H.D. Davis, A.F.C., *British Airways* (1934), *Great Flights* (1935), and *"Let's Learn to Fly!"* (1937). He took a full course of flying instruction at Brooklands Aero Club to equip him to write flying handbooks. For these books he used his real name.

Christopher Sprigg's first post after his return to London was as editor of *British Malaya* (May 1926 – January 1928). This journal was the official organ of the Association of British Malaya, and he contributed editorials and occasional articles. In 1927, however, he had also joined his brother in establishing the aeronautical publishing company Airways Publications Ltd. Christopher and Theodore had invested much of their personal capital in this enterprise and Christopher worked hard on this and another company of which Theodore was director, the Air Press Agency. The magazine *Airways* was produced by Airways Publications. Christopher also wrote advertising copy for Aeromarine Advertising Ltd., where he became Managing Director. Eventually he was made a director of both Airways Publications Ltd and the Air Press Agency. When Airways Publications went bankrupt at the end of 1933, he learned some painful lessons in the more unpleasant side of business competition. Paul Beard (in an interview with the editor, November 1985) suggested that these lessons may have set him questioning seriously for the first time the nature of capitalist economics.

Throughout these years Christopher had engaged in an extraordinary range of literary and other intellectual pursuits. Although he published only two short poems during his lifetime[2] poetry-writing was the activity to which he always gave priority. He worked at poetry, as he did at everything else, in short intense bursts. Hundreds of poems were produced in this way, and he continually typed up selections from his work ready for publication.

Between January and March 1933 Theodore and Christopher Sprigg were joint editors of *Work and Opportunities: The National Advertiser of British Industry Training and Service* which ran for only twelve weekly issues, but Christopher wrote regular copy for this journal. During the same period *Crime in Kensington*, a detective novel by C. St. John Sprigg, was published, the first of eight pot-boilers to appear between 1933 and 1937. His only serious novel, *This My Hand*, came out in 1936. Many short stories were written too, but none of these was published in Christopher's lifetime.

His interest in technology and engineering extended from aviation to motor-cars. In 1929, in *Automobile Engineer* XIX, he had published theoretical notes on possible improvements in the design of automatic gears. The following year he patented a design for a new kind of variable speed gear. In his *Biographical Note* to the *Poems* (1939) Paul Beard recalled that these ideas attracted considerable attention at the time, notably from the famous automobile engineer, Sir Harry Ricardo, though nothing tangible seems to have come from the invention. It was as a theorist that Christopher Sprigg excelled in the study of physics. *The Crisis in Physics*, published in 1939 in an edition by Professor H. Levy, is obviously unfinished work, but there is enough completed material, especially in the early chapters, to show its author's sophisticated views about the nature of the physical world and the development of our Western understanding of it.

By the end of 1934 Christopher Sprigg had decided to make writing a full-time career. In a letter to Paul Beard on 21 December 1934 he described his workload during a period when he had written much new verse, his first serious novel, and several short stories:

> Also during the last three months I have written the following tripe; 1 Detective Novel. 1 Aviation text-book. 30 aviation articles. 6 detective short stories. Heaven knows how many news paragraphs. Done 4 half-days a week office work.

The quickly dashed off detective novels (sometimes written within a fortnight) were reasonably successful in commercial terms, and he now intended that they should keep him in funds while he devoted his time to the more serious matter of writing poetry, stories, and theoretical studies.

He seems to have been an unusually earnest young man, though neither friendless nor without a sense of humour. He had girl friends but never came near to a permanent relationship with any of them, and he lived harmoniously with Theodore both before and after his elder brother's marriage. He seems always to have been on good terms with his elder sister Paula who became a Roman Catholic nun and taught in the convent school which she had attended as a girl. His family and friends tell of his strong sense of fun, revealed particularly in stories which he told against himself. Paul Beard relates one of these: "His story of being thrown when riding in Windsor Park is typical: 'The horse arrived back wearing my wrist-watch'." His half-sister Rosemary Sprigg reports her mother's story of an occasion when, having just moved to a new flat, there was a mild family squabble. Trying to make a dignified and cool withdrawal from the room Christopher walked straight inside a small broom cupboard. He emerged smiling, mocking his previous attitude of self-importance.

Towards the end of 1934 he began a serious reading of Marxist writings, including Marx and Engels, Lenin, Stalin, and other Russian Marxists. Paul Beard, his closest friend at that time, believes that this interest in politics and Marxism emerged quite suddenly, though Christopher plunged himself with his usual concentrated vigour into this new activity. During the next two years he wrote the essays which were published after his death as *Studies in a Dying Culture* (1938), *Further Studies in a Dying Culture* (1949), and *Romance and Realism* (1979) as well as his books *Illusion and Reality* (1937) and *The Crisis in Physics* (1939). He wrote many poems too, but they were completed in dwindling gaps between the writing of Marxist-inspired studies of modern Western culture and regular activity on behalf of the Communist Party. Christopher joined the Poplar branch of the Party in London's East End – where he lived for a time – in late 1935 or early 1936. He became Secretary for the branch on 31 March 1936, and took a part in the routine activities of a Communist cell in the 1930s. He helped to spread party propaganda by fly-posting bills, selling copies of the *Daily Worker*, and speaking at public street-corner meetings.

On 11 December 1936 the Poplar branch purchased an ambulance for the Republican cause in Spain, and Christopher volunteered to drive it to the front-lines. He became a member of the International Brigade and joined a convoy driving across France. On arrival in Spain he became a machine-gun instructor and edited his battalion's Wall Newspaper. Meanwhile his brother Theodore was making determined efforts to have Christopher recalled to England. He showed a proof copy of *Illusion and Reality* to senior Communist Party members in London. Because Christopher had deliberately avoided the leading party intellectuals this was the first they knew of his gifts. They ordered his recall, but it was too late. On 24 January Christopher wrote from Albacete that action was near. On the afternoon of 12 February 1937 his section fought its first battle against some of Franco's Moorish troops on a hill near the Jarama River, outside Madrid, and Christopher was killed.

In his last letter to Paul Beard, on 9 December 1936, just before he set out for Spain, Christopher Sprigg wrote: "There is always the possibility that I may not come back from Spain, in which case I shall leave behind me a mass of manuscript some of which may be worth publishing." He then listed some of this possibly worthwhile work, singling out *Studies in a Dying Culture* which, he noted, "was only drafts but with some good ideas" and *The Crisis in Physics*, half of which was ready for the press, the other half written but requiring revision "for grammar and sense". He was more diffident about his short stories and poems which "all belong to my dishonest and sentimental past" though parts, he thought, were worth publishing. His plays and novels, however, were "all completely worthless". All the manuscripts had been left with Theodore but, Christopher emphasised (the underlining is his) "with the understanding that he is <u>guided by you</u>."

Christopher Sprigg's choice of Paul Beard as literary arbiter on his behalf was neither sudden nor casual. Beard had been the closest audience and critic for Christopher's writing from the summer of 1930 when Christopher sent him copies of "The Art of Dying", the "Smoke and Diamond" sequence, and other early pieces. Beard, with his first wife, Elizabeth, read all the work which Christopher thought of as "serious" as soon as he had written it. The Beards encouraged him and they were not afraid to tell him when they thought his poems, stories, and essays bad. Though he did not always agree with their judgements – especially after he entered his Marxist phase – it is obvious from his letters to them that he always trusted the Beards and relied upon the careful honesty of their criticism.

Paul Beard's selection of poems from the manuscripts which appeared in 1939 as *Poems* by Christopher Caudwell confirms the wisdom of Christopher's faith in Beard's judgement. Apart from "The Art of Dying" (written in 1926 but much revised thereafter) and five short "juvenilia", the poems published in this first collection were written at the end of 1934 or early in 1935. They are: "The Hair"; "Hymn to Philosophy"; "Tierra del Fuego"; "Was It?"; "Donne's Reverie"; "The Stones of Ruskin"; "Classic Encounter"; "The Progress of Poetry"; "Essay on Freewill"; "The Coal"; "Twenty Sonnets of Wm. Smith"; "The Art of Dying", and the long dramatic poem *Orestes. Poems* – with the exception of the "juvenilia" (which are to be found in the first section – Early Poems) – constitute Section 3 of the present volume

What strikes the reader at once about Christopher Sprigg's poems is their lack of *literary* sophistication. Even in these later poems – and despite the Donne-inspired witty style of two of them – very little of the writing shows any consistent debt to the inventions of literary modernism. He was an autodidact who shunned the literary cliques and fashions of the 1930s as completely as he did the orthodoxies of Communist Party intellectualism. Unlike other notable autodidacts – Thomas Hardy and Dylan Thomas, for example – he did not have in his adolescence the sort of education which can be transmitted by a revered older person steeped in literature. The result is self-made poetry with some of the stilted earnestness, gaucheness, and occasional bathos which untrained literary independence can entail.

Christopher had read fairly widely in poetry. There are echoes of Thomas Hardy, Robert Graves, Rupert Brooke, and Wilfred Owen, for example, in his early poems, and of Shakespeare, Skelton, and other British poets. But no one writer's influence permanently modified his poetic development. There is no clear line of development in his technique, either, though later poems are usually easily distinguished from earlier. A longer formal education in literature might have produced greater consistency of style, but his intellectual restlessness would have resisted any concentration of that kind.

His habit of taking poetry up in "bouts of inspiration" – as he termed them – was as much a matter of temperament as of the necessity imposed by his many commercial commitments and other literary activities. Nevertheless the poems have a genuineness, an urgent and serious honesty which makes the reader attend to their plain language and simple forms and rhythms. And when he does so, the reader hears the restless and distinctive questionings of a sophisticated twentieth-century mind.

Honesty and sophistication appear in many ways. He saw with modern unvarnished bleakness, for example, how art does not protect one from the sort of madness which found John Ruskin in his old age; nor does it protect from the ravages of age:

> The wisest stop their gambols and become
> As ease stops up the operative glands
> Sleek, ox-eyed, ruminative gelded beasts
> Or at the worst drift off the stage of life
> The slobber-lipped and palsied clowns of age.
> All others come to curse the thing they blessed
> And daub their chains with filth or scream at night,
> Whipped by all the fat devils out of hell
> Until their brother-madmen stop their mouths.
> ("The Stones of Ruskin")

He saw too, in "The Progress of Poetry", the hurts of psychological repression as sharply and vividly as Blake did:

> I saw a Gardener with a watering can
> Sprinkling dejectedly the heads of men
> Buried up to their necks in the wet clay.
>
> I saw a Bishop born in sober black
> With a bewildered look on his small face
> Being rocked in a cradle by a grey-haired woman.

> I saw a man, with an air of painful duty
> Binding his privates up with bunches of ribbon.
> The woman who helped him was decently veiled in white.

The nightmare and surreal quality of the poem's opening is developed throughout, and it ends:

> The Gardener answered: "I am more vexed by the lichen
> Upon my walls. I scraped it off with a spade.
> As I did so I heard a very human scream.
>
> "In evening's sacred cool, among my bushes
> A figure was wont to walk. I deemed it angel.
> But look at the footprint. There's hair between the toes!"

The thorny philosophical problem of process- and time-bound man's freedom is translated into other nightmarish images, and a telling final couplet in "Essay on Freewill":

> Our vain regrets are dinosaurs
> Infesting coalseams of the hours
> Our hopes as fast as time can spin
> Pressed up in calf-bound books like flowers.
>
> Remember me when I am dead
> The last thing that Napoleon said.

Much of the work in *Poems* exhibits a mood of unsentimental realism, especially about sexual relationships ("The Coal" and "The Hair", for example). The Christopher Sprigg of 1935 rejected his sentimental and idealist past. In "Hymn to Philosophy" he addressed the "swamp foul", traditional Western Idealism:

> I have caressed your sort, I must confess,
> But give me beauty beauty that must end
> And rots upon the taxidermist's hands.

Most of the poems in the collection also convey an original mind at work in spite of its limited literary means. But it is in the two longest sequences in *Poems* – "Twenty Sonnets of Wm. Smith" and *Orestes* – that we find both more apparent formal conventionality and most actual originality. "The Sonnets of Wm. Smith" in which modern love is seen freed from illusion – recount a love-affair in which sexuality is satisfaction of physical need, in which the loved one is far from perfect, and all notions of mystical union are renounced. The renunciation is sometimes fierce, as in the revolutionary sonnet VI;

> Lift the church and find the altar;
> Lift the altar; find the stone:
> Lift the stone and find the toad;
> Lift the toad and find the rock.
>
> I heaved the rock up, heaved like hell,
> I pulled the rock up by the roots;
> I pulled a church up by the hair:
> Church and altar; stone and toad.
>
> We found the occupation childish,
> And while the organ, solemn, godlike,
> Pealed out of the stained-glass windows
> We fornicated to its tune.
> Jones, more mystic, with a groan
> Bashed his brains out on the stone.

The sequence ends with the hope that a new honest sexuality may become the subject of song, as it was before the dawn of the Christian era:

> Yes, even the wood's great pimp the nightingale
> In the full flood of meretricious song
> Set on by his unholy bawd the moon
> May be permitted to observe our love
> And sing of it, no more a leering foe,
> As once he used, two thousand years ago.
>
> ("Sonnet XX")

Orestes does not have the energy and verbal panache of Auden and Isherwood's *The Dog Beneath the Skin* (1935) or *The Ascent of F6* (1936), but it is surprising that this verse drama is not played more often – at least as a play for voices. It is both serious and funny, its ironic and playful surface barely holding down its depths of pain, bewilderment, and grief. *Orestes*, at one time given the more interesting title *Orestes in Harley Street*, is a farewell to the illusions of mythic psychology. It parallels the discussion of Freud as bourgeois and mythic psychologist in *Studies in a Dying Culture*. At the end of *Orestes*, but too late for the guilt-ridden Orestes and Electra who have been haunted to hysterical self-destruction by the visitations of Furies, Shades, and the ghosts of Clytemnestra and Agamemnon, Athene descends to proclaim:

> But as for you, you shades or Furies, go!
> You're merely inhibited tendencies
> And now I've analysed you, quick, avaunt!
> You see? They've gone. Do what you want to do.

But it is the voices of the man-constructed Furies and of the dead, rehearsing the modern evils and perils of human existence, which echo longest in memory:

> We have published a monograph on trophallaxis
> Exhibiting the human parasite:
> Its sexual habits and autophagy,
> Its aberrance, self-mutilation, fits.
> We are proudest of our patented man-poison
> Which will not make a stench. It's guaranteed.
> It is secreted in the pest's intestines.
> He drinks; it swells; he crawls away and dies.

Only the immortal gods assume the comic and detached stance which our human situation merits. *Orestes* is Christopher Sprigg's finest single poetic achievement partly because it so eloquently gives the lie to easy optimism about or pat solutions to the problems of the human condition in our time. Its honesty may be a reason why it has never been much used as political propaganda.

The poems published here for the first time in book form have been selected from a large quantity of manuscript material. Most of this is now held by the Humanities Research Centre in the University of Texas at Austin. A fuller description of this material may be found in the *Notes* (page 179). Many other drafts and manuscript early versions of the poems as well as a few poems not to be found in any other state elsewhere are currently in the possession of the Sprigg family. As far as possible the latest draft or version of any poem has been included here. Christopher Sprigg sometimes made extensive later alterations to particular poems in a sequence – to the "Smoke and Diamond" sequence, originally written in 1926, for example. In such instances I have invariably adopted the latest version, even if this creates an imbalance of tone or diction between the altered poem and other poems in the sequence. From time to time Christopher Sprigg made up collections for publication, notably one of early poems – to which he gave the title *The Assignation and Other Poems*, probably in 1927 – and another, towards the end of his life, which he called *Point of Departure*. A large number of the poems chosen for *The Assignation* appear now in the first section (Early Poems) and, with the addition of several extra pieces, the poems chosen by him for *Point of Departure* make up the second section and provide its title.

This *Collected Poems* does not attempt to be a complete edition of Christopher Sprigg's poetry. From the large quantity of early poems – those composed between 1921 and 1927 – I have selected work which has either thematic or technical interest. In 1924 and 1925 Christopher Sprigg turned his skills to the art of translation, producing stylish English versions of over a hundred epigrams from the Greek Anthology and of many of Horace's Odes. For the Greek translations – as for his versions of Chinese poems – he made use of literal cribs in English. A small number of these early translations – all of them selected by Christopher Sprigg himself at some time – may be found in all three sections.

Over many years he struggled to complete an elegiac sequence for the dead of World War I. This seems to have started as a "Requiem Mass" for 11 November 1921. Its title was changed frequently, and the sequence grew. By the time it was abandoned it had become "November the Eleventh", and pious patriotism had become more sceptical (though never cynical). There are touches of anger at times. One early version of "The Consecration" ends:

> They shall not see again the emperor sun
>   Nor know the air's caress;
> Mankind is only unimportant dust
>   Defiled with foolishness.
> But all Creation stands and stares this day,
>   The bare sky stoops to bless
> Aghast, but eager to behold confirmed
>   Faith's endless steadfastness.

In the final version there are some telling substitutions and omissions (including the echo of W.H. Davies's "Leisure"):

> And as they cannot see the emperor sun
>   Nor know the air's caress,
> The mind of man, this dedicated day
>   Ceases its business
> Amused, yet strengthened to behold approved
>   Faith's unwise steadfastness.

Two other rather strange poems about the war – "The Assignation; 1916" and "The Firing Party: 1917" – were also written quite soon after Christopher had left school. The first is addressed to an enemy, killer or victim. The second is the thoughts of a soldier about to be shot for cowardice. Both poems appear in several versions and seem to have been constantly reconsidered.

Another sequence, "Smoke and Diamond", was composed in 1926 when Christopher was going through an intense religious phase. The language here is sometimes stilted and abstract, but the feeling genuine. The simplicity and strength recall George Herbert's in poems such as "The Pulley", and sometimes there is a gentle wit like that found in Herbert too. "Complexity" begins:

> This soul of mine, for all its scurrying thoughts,
>   Deep-diving memory, and yawing will,
> Is but a child's simplicity of noughts
>   By body's babel – even when it's still.
>
> Mechanic sinews, living bone, pleached nerves,
>   Republic by some rare refinement knit
> Into a sudden clap of shimmering curves
>   A moment – then earth drinks up all of it.

The section also contains one or two interesting separate lyrics – including the fantasy "The Sick Bed", which recreates the fever-fed imaginative journey of a mind – and a small group of short love lyrics.

The pieces which most justify this new expanded edition of Christopher Sprigg's poetry are included in its second section. Some of the poems in this section were assembled by him – probably in 1934 or 1935 – as likely material for the volume he projected as *Point of Departure*. Some of the poems exist in more than one version and where this is the case an attempt has been made to identify the latest version.

The "Point of Departure" section contains a variety of lyric poems, several of them more personally revealing than those in Paul Beard's *Poems* (1939); some are engagingly confessional and self-critical – "The Survival", for example. Although there are earlier poems – including more of the translations from the Greek Anthology and the poem "Once I Did Think" (now re-titled "The Ecstasy") which was published in *Dial* in March 1927 – most of the work clearly dates from the 1930s. It shows the thought of a man in transition between the contemplative ritual of romantic heroism and existential preparation for action, between – as Christopher Sprigg termed it – illusion and reality. But it is not simply the "illusion" of bourgeois idealism set against the "reality" of Marxism. Christopher Sprigg's family and professional background were conducive to action in the social world. As D.E.S. Maxwell suggested in his *Poets of the Thirties* (1969):

> For Christopher's family the arts as well as being a private pleasure had, so to speak, a technical interest. The business of journalism and editing kept them closer to general society than the coterie world of the intellectuals. Ideological fashions blow strongest in the rarefied Oxbridge air.... He was born into, in a sense, a nomad tradition, ready to pursue unfamiliar tracks: a family with a wide circle of friends gathered from many places; a profession familiar with the medium of words serving a variety of intellectual purposes.[3]

The poems written during the 1930s confirm this view. There are waspish epigrams directed against politicians and sundry establishment figures, in much the same tone as the more satirical pieces from the Greek Anthology. A growing quarrel with religion and idealist philosophies is a subject of many poems, including "The Consolations of Religion", "The Unspeakables", "The Last Judgement", and "The Kingdom of Heaven". Idealism of a sort is allowed to answer back, too, in poems such as "The Danger", where he addresses a spiritual teacher (possibly Christ) who has "seduced me into virtues / where I shall drown". Other poems explore candidly the nature of his poetic talent and its possible direction, as in "Poet's Invocation" and a poem simply titled "To –" which ends:

> How did you get that trick of writing verse?
> Mine melt upon the palate without pain,
> As bland as the post-prandial cigarette,
> As null. No reader has coughed blood for me...

His religious faith abandoned, he now discovers a new feeling of emptiness and isolation, as in "The Audience":

> The Gods go one by one and leave me lonely.
> The stars of heaven nudge one another, snigger,
> And go about their business. I remain
> And hear the fire of youth sink in the grate,
> New tenants cachinnating on the doorstep,
> Rats in the loft, and from the family vaults
> Ancestral voices prophesying trouble.

In "The Nature of the Physical Universe" Time proclaims his total boredom with the universe and the poet too seems to announce the death and rediscovery of poetic imagination:

> "That's the end, and in my view –
> And I've been stage-manager here since the beginning –
> They might as well walk out and close the box-office."
> And he slammed the lid of his trunk with a spiteful bang;
> While far away, down on the pavement, I heard
> The click of clockwork and a throaty song
> As urchin fingers found the nightingale.

The language is generally simple, colloquial, and direct. One of the few love-poems, "The Secret", is an admirably deft renunciation of a love relationship. There are some ambitious exercises. "Sales Pastoral" evokes Spring in the language of contemporary commerce, and "Kensington Rime" is an attractive zany piece of home-made surrealism in which Coleridge's Ancient Mariner has become Miss Miffin who once slew a brightly coloured bird in Kensington. After many strange adventures Miss Miffin learns a hypothetical and tautological truth through the messages of Rosie relayed through a not-very-reliable fairground medium:

> And oft as doth the day return
>   Of my forgiven crime
> I stop the first young man I meet
>   And tell him all in rime.
>
> I teach him Rosie's childish prayer
>   So simple and so sweet
> If to do good were to do good
>   Then to do good were meet.

There is no punctuation in "Kensington Rime", evidence that it was a deliberate exercise in modernist poetics.

Christopher Sprigg's love of heroes and heroic adventure is most apparent in two of the poems. "Polar Exploration" (not a part of the planned *Point of Departure* volume) was written around 1929 or 1930. Once again, as in his poems for the heroes of World War I, he writes very seriously and conventionally, as though he finds inventiveness slightly inhibited by his awe at his subject. A later poem, "In Memoriam T.E. Shaw", has some of the same awkwardness. Lawrence of Arabia – the subject of a critically sympathetic study of the bourgeois hero in *Studies in a Dying Culture*[4] – is treated with some reverence in this elegy which must have been written in 1935, the year in which Lawrence was killed in a motor-cycle accident. The poem comes close at times to bathos:

> Hail and farewell! We wish you, slain by chance,
> The comfort of this last irrelevance.
> Hail! for you raced conjecture from the start,
> But as for faring well, you lacked the art;

And yet the poem is a subtle portrait too of the man who, as T.E. Shaw, sought anonymity and escape from his Lawrence of Arabia persona. The poem's ending is rhetorical, witty, and moving:

> You who of all found the most hardly won
> What most men own by birth – oblivion,
> But now at last secured, as without thanks
> You ply some menial office in death's ranks,
> And undistinguished service that supplies
> The sombre livery of your last disguise.

"Heil Baldwin!" – a poem of 642 lines – was Christopher Sprigg's only Communist poem, indeed his only overtly political poem. As with the elegy for T.E. Lawrence we are able to date the poem by its references to actual events – in this case the signing of the Naval Agreement between Britain and Germany in 1935. It is quite effective political satire, passionately indignant. It is odd that it was not published at the time, in *Left Review* for example. Rhythmically rather monotonous, as such political satires invariably seem to be, it has many telling couplets and turns of phrase; he lampoons Goering with relish, for example:

> Goering, who it would be unjust to say
> Was nothing but a bully in decay,
> A loudmouthed barrel fired with drugs and drink,
> Able to bellow, strut, all things but think,
> Who had but one idea his life long –
> That he was of importance – and that wrong.

But in the end the poem falls short of greatness because much is simply propaganda, with all the crude emotionalism of the genre:

> Still, underground, forbidden papers pass
> And voice the wrongs of the exploited class;
> Still Lenin's wisdom and the thoughts of Marx
> Burn steadily, and spread, and send up sparks,
> And this time, suddenly as the Reichstag fright,
> No building, but a people see alight!

The poem presents the contemporary reader with a further difficulty. Radical changes have taken place in our historical knowledge and interpretation of the poem's central incident – the Reichstag Fire of 27 February 1933, which event was instrumental in the Nazi seizure of power in Germany. Modern research has demonstrated quite conclusively[5] that the Nazis had nothing to do with the burning of the Reichstag. Nor was it a Communist plot as the Nazis believed. It appears to have been the single-handed work of the unfortunate deranged Dutch Communist Marinus van der Lubbe who was found guilty after a much-publicised trial lasting almost two months and was executed in January 1934. Like everyone else, however, Christopher Sprigg could not have known the true facts about the Reichstag Fire in 1935 or 1936 when he wrote "Heil Baldwin!" All the available evidence – including the testimony of his poetry – shows that Christopher Sprigg was a free spirit who would have been the first to mock his own ignorance. The artist, he believed, is a self-maker as much as he is a maker of art. Art does not exist, however, for the sake of "self-expression". On the contrary:

> The value of art to the artist then is this, that it makes him free. It appears to him of value as a self-expression, but in fact it is not the expression of a self but the discovery of a self. In synthesizing experience with society's, in pressing his inner self into the mould of social relations, he not only creates a new mould, a socially valuable product, but he also moulds and creates his own self. The mute inglorious Milton is a fallacy. Miltons are made not born.[6]

These *Collected Poems* are more than a documentation in self-making, however. They are the work of a poet who was continually developing, and they show that Christopher Sprigg's early death signified a loss for English poetry as much as for the more imaginative reaches of intellectual life generally.

ALAN YOUNG

Notes

[1] G.S. Fraser, *The Modern Writer and his World* (revised edition), Harmondsworth, Penguin Books, 1964, p.382.

[2] "Once I Did Think" appeared in *Dial* LXXXII, 3 March 1927, p.187, signed Christopher Sprigg. See "The Ecstasy", p.87. "High on a bough beneath the moonlight pale" was published in *The Saturday Review*, 4 May 1929, p.610, signed Albert. See p.69.

[3] D.E.S. Maxwell, *Poets of the Thirties*, London, Routledge & Kegan Paul, 1969, p.64.

[4] Christopher Caudwell, *Studies in a Dying Culture*, London, John Lane The Bodley Head, 1938, pp.20-43.

[5] See Fritz Tobias, *The Reichstag Fire: Legend and Truth*. Translated from the German by Arnold J. Pomerans. With an Introduction by A.J.P. Taylor. London, Secker & Warburg, 1963.

[6] Christopher Caudwell, in "D.H. Lawrence: A Study of the Bourgeois Artist", *Studies in a Dying Culture*, London, John Lane The Bodley Head, 1938, p.53.

Early Poems
1924-1927

SONNET ON HIS 17TH BIRTHDAY

I wished, ere I should see this lagging year
With Helen's breasts and Caesar's coronal
To carve some Memphian answer to your call;
But now, what with my weariness and fear
For potence, not the fact, I seize God's ear;
For I see rosy works feed Death, and all
The intricate sweets Spring's practised hand can rear
Are not a name before the first snows fall,

Art! golden bird, my fain feet fled you after!
Yet a great Voice rang, "See how your Years flee
For Tideless God grinds down Time's iron shore.
Knock; seek and find!" – rang through forced tears and laughter.
Lord. Lord, my groping knuckles find no door.
Way, seek my feet! Refuge, come thou to me.

October 20th, 1924

EASTER THOUGHTS FROM SUMMER

I saw the drifts of daffodils
And poppies yawning on the hills:
Such overplus as late Spring spills
On Summer till her hot lap fills.

Ah God! I have played false! What shame
Seeing those drowsed vistas came!
Thou has forgot; thou hast forgot.
Here thy vow was; and now is not!

How soon I have put by thy woes!
Two months, and earth among her snows
Could not find violet or young rose
To wreathe thy death-besweated Brows!

And now – yea, God I have forgot –
But lo, I am, and I am not:
And all my days betwixt would seem
Like language uttered in a dream

Save through star-crashes Thou hold me,
While, as the sun's orbed majesty
Dies lonely on a darkling sea
Time sets into Eternity.

ON "A PUBLIC SCHOOL ANTHOLOGY"

Are these the lays of the young Lord of Day?
If sing you must, why not in your own tongue
Music you surely knew – the summer sun
In glory dying past the playing fields
While the wet grass breathes its keen evening smell
On the cool breezes; the unvext clear pool
That takes the body like Sleep's wings; the pit
And breasted tape; and all those quiet hours
In some lush meadow with a friend and book
Till twilight was felt crouched in the deep vales
Then walked the hills. And slowly we returned
Tired; and each lonely lad heard the old call
Of Honour racing with the wind of Death,
Could you forget so easily, or not know,
That should you ape in sickly predecease
Our own just-dying song; that you should strive
To imp your feathers on our broken wings?
And must you speak in feigned tones ever to tell
Of how there smote your suddenly-dreamy eyes
The gleam of Aphrodite's brilliant flesh,
Uncaved from her shell which lay beneath all storm,
Rising; gold hair blown round her blue-veined breasts
On the dark seas, to hide her girdle's glint.

BIOGRAPHIES

Because men's lives are brief they toil
    To set an earmark on the days;
    And chart the estate of starry ways
(Though all their entail is some soil): –

"My house was founded by that sun
    And with the mists shut out the skies;"
    Or, "Ere the unlidding violets' eyes
My book was planned, attempted, done."

And love; so that love's hot lips laid
    Upon the cheek of life's own noon
    May make more separate the moon
Which drowns in deeps of silent shade.

Had Man all Time for his domain
    He'd reel, stupid with liberty,
    The helix of Eternity
In seasons round and round again;

While primroses appeared; while lean
    Grew kine with heat; while sunset glows
    Lit leaves; while all the land was snows;
While once again the ways were clean.

THE MOUND (BRADFORD "LAYS")

Sole stretch of earth uncoveted by man
Here, the huge mound rears a brown rugged head:
No green thing lives upon this height, unfed
Save by the chance-caught soil of soot and air
Smoke- and sweat-smelling, air here nigh Life's ban;
And back to back through the cracked houses stare,
Crushed close as twisted roofs and sagged walls can,
The sheer, hard lump bears neither house nor shed.

Yet – steep and broken brick strewn – in a land
Where dirt and dung spatter the narrow streets,
This is the grimed oasis where boys stand
Or kick the stones; where neighbour neighbour greets.
Here, bulked beneath the mills its cause and warden,
The common playground lies, their plantless garden.

TRANSLATION OF CATULLUS'S "VIVAMUS, MEA LESBIA"

My Lesbia, let us live and love,
And at one farthing, not above
Rate all the talk of crabbed old men.
Suns may set, and rise again:
The sleep of an eternal night
Is ours, when sets our little light.
Let's kiss! When we've a thousand had,
A hundred, then a thousand add.
Then give a hundred kisses more,
A thousand, and a hundred o'er!
Then, with so many thousands kissed
We'll get confused and lose the list,
For fear of envious spells from such
As know our kisses were so much.

AGNOSIS

If you are Way and Light, O show more clearly
    The road, the gate.
Speak, speak! Else can a mortal know thee
    How good and great?
Wearily, wearily comes back the answer
    "Child, I can wait.

For I am the doubt to thee as to others
    I am the Faith.
The Light to them, but to thee, in the shadows
    Lurk I, a wraith.
The Way to them – but seek thou me in the forest,"
    The voice saith.

"I come not when zephyrs beneath a hot heaven
    Shake bee and flower;
But when o'er the wings of the daystar folded
    Gloomy clouds tower;
When the tired wings sing naught but 'Evening! Evening!',
    That is my hour."

ON A DEAD CAT

Your proud-held head's forever laid
On earth, in death, not sleep. You're made
Such sight as you would have disdained –
A matted carcase, gravel-stained.
No more, life-still, on days death-still,
You'll bask and drowse upon the sill,
Or stroke yourself against my chair
With spread-out paws and tail in air,
Or, purring, press your soft round head
Into my palm; for you are dead.

Good-bye! Ere I could come, disease
Conquered at last beneath your trees,
You, who affected pride of race
And warmth; but most unfailing grace
In sleep; night-hunting through the woods;
And the sea-changes of your moods.

IN THE AEGEAN

We passed that day on the Aegean deep,
   Those lovely children of the Cyclades,
And thought of all the gracious forms that sleep,
   Prisoned in rock, beside those tuneful seas,
Never to be released! for in the dust
   The enchanted chisels of Phidias rust.

ON DRYDEN

He made the eyes of Logic glow,
   His curse anticipated Fate.
His serene justice to his foe
   Adds to the list of virtues, hate.

from THE PROGRESS OF POETRY

1

While still wrapt in Unreason's night,
  Or yet were active, Mind and Will,
My sponsors fixt, with solemn rite,
  My signature to baptism's Bill,
    Whereby was cheaply purchased
    The Blood which our Redeemer shed.

Now winter stealeth o'er my prime
  Wherein falls the due date I fear,
Which I must honour in strict time,
  Nor 'vaileth treasure laid up here;
    For Death, the cashier, reckoneth not
    Such wealth as moth and mildew rot.

Some little store I have above,
  Earned not by merit but of Grace;
Only my Lord's abounding love
  Can fill my coffers in that place.
    Still aid, Lord! lest, poor sinner, I
    Be Grace's bankrout when I die!

2

Despite the anguished scream of will,
  Habit still its compulsion wreaks
To shrink the flesh upon the bone
  And bleach the hair with plague streaks.

Keats has observed the nightingale
  And others bayed the moon of verse,
And subtle logics out of ten
  Equations built the Universe.

We too in our far humbler way
  Have known the philosophic thrill
Of intellect, an instrument
  To modulate the wind of will.

Yet look! flesh rots upon our bones,
  Defying reason's mastery,
While callow youth in our house room
  Battens on our sagacity....

Well, they are of our tainted seed,
  And shall achieve our present stage
Only to feel crawl in their blood
  The grey bacteria of age.

SICK BED

He thought of childhood's village bright as glass
  In ripeness lapsing whither it was wrung –
The path's quaint paving gnawed by the tough grass,
  Moss on the tiles, and the walls rambler-hung.

The great tea-roses slept, the hollyhocks
  Were shedding their bloom-caverns steadily;
The individual woodbine-heads with shocks
  From kind marauders waved in a slow sea.

Now he was gone inside: upon the land
  The sunlight lay like an old god at rest;
But inwards shafted, and its drowsy hand
  Beat with a cry at the intruder's breast.

The room and dusk hung like a cube of lead
  Upon him; tho' his body was a mesh
Of signals he could not move hand or head.
  An unseen devil caught his jerking flesh

And cold air crept along it. He was flying
  And all the room swung too: from far he heard
The clock's harsh blows were paused. In space half-dying
  He lay with all his burden; not a word –

Not a word that crawled embryo in his brain
  Could win its weight or substance: then he screamed,
And all his flesh obeyed his soul again;
  Awoke, and thro' the sunlight porch he streamed

Over the garden.... For a little while
    He haunted well-known places – like the downs
A humming peace broad-curved for mile on mile,
    With chalk rubbed through upon their turfy crowns.

And that retreat, those water-bright green meadows
    Which nursed a streamlet in their broken ground;
Thro' reedy clumps it glides, but never shadows
    With small pale blue forget-me-nots around.

The giant chestnuts drowned; the patchwork downs
    Were silent as a church, for it was noon;
The forest-clouds were mottled now with browns,
    But no leaf fell where thousands would fall soon.

But he was gone away; the golden sun
    Had washed out the rich landscape, mist on mist,
And then the sunlight and himself were one,
    As Life and Death in that bright ocean kissed.

FROM THE GREEK

1

O would I were a red rose that, blooming where your feet go,
I might be plucked by your fingers and laid in your breast of snow!

2

O would I were as the wind that, walking where the seas flow,
You might lay your bosom and receive me as I blow!

ON A NOVELIST

    She would have been quite flawless, like pure glass,
    But through her soul she let the world's light pass.

THE STRANGER

Within your soul the woman plays
   Parts learned in lives bygone,
And from your eyes a stranger's gaze
In me the man's peculiar ways
   Watches more than my own.

And, dreaming, I see in your eyes
   The quintessential you
To dawns more bright austerely rise,
While woman in their fervour dies
   And love begins anew.

MAY

Spring's snow, the hawthorn's in each lane;
   And though the Druids haunt no grove,
Though fairies and rewards are gone,
   Arise and come a-maying, love!

The flowers you lightly pull evoke
   A country ghost, who watched their fall,
Then sang, youth should enjoy its days
   Ere, like the wind, age drink them all.

Ere, like the wind, time devours all
   And runs their husks across the grass,
And cheerly underneath the boughs
   The voices of the centuries pass.

THE RECOLLECTION

Far off eternal sunsets sweep
Skies circling pastures bland and boon;
The hours dance to the heaven's tune,
The fields are bathed in dewy sleep.

Not to that kingdom can I win
While dearer than delight or peace
Your words, your actions, still increase
Love stronger far than death or sin.

Long since I left, not to return,
My watch-tower in the sky of prayers,
Only a vagrant from those airs
A moment made heart bleed and burn.

THE CAPTIVE

O'er-tyrannised by circumstance
   I lie, helpless though hale;
She lives far off from any lance
   Of knight in fairy tale.

Spellbound this idiot hero lies
   The spell – a hair, a flower,
A nothing – fast that warrior ties
   In the unbolted tower.

Ay, stronger than his timid heart,
   Though chivalry protest,
The spell is – laced with magic art
   Through sinews of his breast.

AUTUMNAL

The brazen shard of autumn
   Glints in blue grass;
With whispering feet, linked lovers
   On stiff leaves pass.

At last the wrangling warriors
   Leave calm the soul;
Lips touched, and breast to bosom –
   This is man's goal.

>   Ah, love! to be the summer!
>   To die! if when
>   The winter foamed and vanished
>   We lived again.

CIRCUMSTANCE

In love I moved as one in dream,
  As one in dream I breathed, I ate,
I did things that did not then seem
  So linked with life, so dear to Fate.

And now in darkened woods I wake
  These things are thorns that, foot and hand,
Have bound me. Love and all must break
  Ere heart and soul as free things stand.

The moon in ancient beauty sails
  In skies that flood the heart with awe,
So old, so wise! but on these vales
  Vainly her influence we would draw.

Vainly like moonstruck wights desire
  The calm, remoteness, splendour high.
The thorn is king here, in the mire,
  And we are subject till we die.

THE OCCASION

>   Thought I, this redly sinking sun,
>   These sunburnt trees that spend
>   Their burden in the plashy dun,
>   Meet for some secret end.
>
>   Else why does something in me cry?
>   Why is my heart elate?
>   Why, panting in the lane, do I
>   Tense for this day's death wait?

For nothing... It's a twice-kept tryst:
   One night by the milestone
You met her in the autumn mist,
   To-night you'll be alone.

THE EXPERIENCE

The hawthorn floods with milk the ways.
Both for its beauty and our May,
   My heart is melancholy and sore –
Because of love that rang not true,
Yet can at times my pain renew.
   I shall be different evermore.

NOVEMBER THE ELEVENTH

The Recollection

Returns the day; and I return.
My mind looks back anxious for truth,
And reminiscently to burn
With the raw suffering of its youth.

That was the climax of our faith: –
Let us admit it, who escaped –
Still on the better bank of death,
Shall we defend the God we shaped,

While smuggled from His Hell they lie
For whom no more the metal throats
Of guns assault the arching sky
Nor calm above, the aircraft floats?

The Confession

I thought but yesterday I could deny
Reason's disgust and Life's indignity
If war with honour filled the stormy sky.

I could imagine soul at last released,
As agony on agony increased,
Enparadised when the bombardment ceased.

Because of this a million young and bright
Who shared with us such radiant hopes of fight
Are now eternal exiles from the light.

The world is nothing better than of old;
Our ancient hates in misery we hold;
The guns, long dumb, pride's shameful death-bell tolled
For those who died and cannot now forgive us.

The Justified

They often thought, "If we do this
   We shall be justified.
We shall not pass from life diminished,
With everything marred, botched, unfinished.
   We shall depart with pride."

The storm beat daily on their heads
   And puffed their best to bits.
Mind ceased from cogitation there,
And every phantasy's despair
   Confounded their five wits.

Grant then to those who stir no more,
   In the last shell-hole mired,
Beyond the range of gas and gun,
The honour that they thought they won,
   The pardon they desired!

The Salvation

Can one through an unhallowed life
   Expatiate in sin,
Yet, falling on the battlefield,
   Salvation's city win?

For doubt's redress recall again
   The setting of the scene.
How, oiled and greased with blood and pain
   Revolved the whole machine.

For an eternal bivouac
   Their shattered ranks they rallied,
Their rifles and their kit to stack;
   They will not be reveille'd.

They were not men, but only soldiers,
   Forgiven in brigades,
Who bring their rifles to their shoulders,
   And march into the shades.

God's Gospel

Deafly God watched. He saw the soldiers rise
And take their medicine with slow-tightening hands –
The mouth fall'n open, glazed and popping eyes,
Cold fingers scrabbling in the reddened sands...

Blindly he watched. And heard the high-pitched screaming
Rise all the night up from the stricken field.
He heard the soldiers moan (for they were dreaming) –
Scraps that the torture of their hearts revealed.

Heartless, He stared. He saw the mouthing mites
Loose hands reluctantly, and go away.
He marked the odd achievement of these nights
– Hour upon hour, to turn young vigour grey...

Now that was long ago. To-day the rain
Renews untiringly a private war.
Cold blows the breeze. The airs are cold again.
The nights are thick. This hides our guiding star.

Therefore from the unannotated script,
I read the gospel of this requiem day.
Clear seemed the import; infamously clipped;
And after it, there is not much to say.

"Thicker than leaves man's generations lie,
And these dead leaves – as any other leaf
That flutters down beneath the lowering sky –
Fester beyond the medicine of belief.

"The seasons murmur and earth's fruits increase.
The individual faces will be gone.
The individual battles next will cease
To be; of many wars this War be one.

"They acted in compulsion of some blind
Current of mind, that nerved them for war's pains.
So move migrating herds; so moved mankind
And so were scattered on the hungry plains."

A Profession

Do we believe? Comfortless is this land
    To which our star has led –
Then balance the account and see what gain
    We got for the war's dead.

The gardens over which they tramped in war
    Are ravaged. Nothing lives.
The most the heavens promise is a crop
    When earth at last forgives.

Why sullenly upon the morning's brow,
    And frightening the birds
Triumphant over the war-havocked wheat
    Heard we these boastful words?

They have made justice meddle with hot blood,
    And friendliness with hate.
They have killed peaceful men only for words
    And forced the hand of Fate.

But when the things of earth are only air
    Their faith will still be faith.
Their sweat and fears will bloom upon earth's corpse,
    A flush outbraving death.

Men dreamed their deeds were carven in time's stone.
   Hope led them, and betrayed.
And yet shall save – in that eternity
   When every grave's re-made.

Immortal courage rules the mortal world,
   The cynosure of stars,
The help of man, a bulwark built of flesh,
   And justified in wars.

The Uniform

The soldier triumphed – shall we say?
Or – the man in the soldier's dress?
Which dignified the martial day?
Which bore the anguish and distress?

Glorious in death the soldiers sleep,
Strong bulwarks of our pastured land.
Their flower, their promise still we weep,
Their bravery we understand.

They have revived the soldier's crest.
They sleep in soldier garb for aye,
The wounds of battle in each breast.
They shall not see a civil day.

They rehabilitated war,
They sanctified the martial dress,
But still that nature we must bar –
The element we cannot bless!

The Conundrum

The bugles blow – the banners fly –
Our lances slant across the sky!
I do not love war – no, not I
   But, goodbye home and hearth.
I know not when I made this vow,
Nor recollect the where or how
But still I must fulfil it now,
   O country of my birth!

Yes, strange – we're not the first to say –
That love – the fiercest in its way –
   This strange compulsion owns.
We who loved home so, cold and pale
Lie, far from any English vale.
Our children languish, our farms fail –
Yet we said – Courage must prevail
   For nothing else atones.

The rocks, that felt our gunners' power,
The stars, that saw our aircraft tower,
Earth, that received our mangled flower,
   Join in the perfect hymn.
Always while black's less fair than white,
And right the unperturbed of might,
The Word may come, the cross of light
Receiving which we must, to-night
   Surrender all to Him.

O God, to see the grass again!
Or watch the Chilterns in the rain,
   Through windows rambler-hung.
We have surrendered this for hell.
We shall surrender life as well.
Yet it was right, yet it was well,
Our darkness has become a bell –
   The Song of Songs is sung.

Singing – "We are great – We shall endure
Beyond the virtuous or the pure."

And, "We are fixed – we shall remain
To outlast the stuff of joy and pain."

And, "We are deathless – we shall be
When history sinks upon time's sea."

Consecration

THE CENOTAPH

"A pagan witness to a pagan hate
   I stand in heathen sign
That no old gods of heathendom nor Christ

    Can make the dead divine.
They are not; they are dead; the earth revolves,
    And the stars shine...

MANSOUL

"They argue that survive. More dignified
    The dead their silence keep
Among the low and useless stones and do not stir
    In death's protracted sleep.

"Earth shall forget them into her dark veins
    And reabsorb their blood.
When the wheat swells and bloated poppies flare
    We shall forget war's mud.

"But in the secret centre of all light
    Faith still will shine
Trimming the fervour wherewith frailty blazed
    To the Divine.

"The mouthless plants that creep towards their food
    The light;
The tender doe that overlooks its young
    Day and night,
The tree that rears, uselessly, incessantly
    Its height –
Faith urges and condones them, blind as them
    Nor sees the end.

"These gave their flesh and blood at faith's request
    Into war's hands,
And they are nothing. They are like a wind
    Stirring Time's sands,
Earth to its ancient devilry returns
    And as it was it stands.

And as they cannot see the emperor sun
    Nor know the air's caress,
The mind of man, this dedicated day
    Ceases its business
Amused, yet strengthened to behold approved
    Faith's unwise steadfastness."

The Dream

I heard a voice from obscure dungeons rising
Out of its prison's terrible chilly darkness,
The voice called – self-possessed, as if advising.
Although no glittering stars relieved sky's starkness,
It touched heaven's vaults with peace, like the moon rising.

I followed it through tombs as black as this
And saw white faces of the souls we slew,
Condemned to feel no more the sunlight's kiss,
Yet eager in life, as I had been, I knew,
To drink the air that sweet and common is.

"Our young endeavour is all nullified.
Much pain was of your wreaking, and distress;
But that I rot here wasted, most hurts pride.
You have quenched my flame with death and uselessness.
Yet touch this hand; and I will be your guide."

I followed, on through vaults beneath the earth,
Where slumber smoked the hollow roof of death.
Poor hooded ghosts, who gave these soldiers birth
Were there; tending their steady flames of breath.
The voice said, "You will tread again the earth.

"Yet you must sleep with us at last; make one
In calm and night, with our reflective band,
And, though you forget us in the noonday sun
In evening's quiet you will understand
The mischief your ferocity has done.

"In evening peace white faces will be near;
And sombre eyes look at you; war return.
You will again tread all the maze of fear,
Your heart with honour's riddle bleed and burn,
Far from your native land, thence held more dear."

The Sign

The world before the war was dull.
   How foolproof honest living seemed!
   The powers of Earth discussed and dreamed.
While Europe's cornet flared to full.

Then battle came in Flanders. Fast
   The harsh glare waxed around Namur,
   But loudly, loudly, glad and sure
Our hearts resounded to war's blast.

For war was in our hearts. And spoken
   Conundrums half-familiar –
   "Ease is a word to make or mar
But there's one word must not be broken!

"Bombardment, thunder on our gates!
   Rain, batter from a smoking sky!
   O humming death bird, float on high,
To sit in judgment on our fates!

"In sweat and pain the Word sustains;
   The spirit quickens in blood's bath.
   Eternal patience crowns our wrath.
We blossom in these barren plains."

       *   *   *

"Well, at the last the thing was done
   And we – we did not alter much,
   Though millions put to the touch
Will never see again the sun.

"We know the thing for which they fought,
   An unborn race cannot inherit;
   They gained no treasure of the spirit;
Nor did they touch the loins of thought.

"Men will make much the same mistakes;
   And they, for all that fire of soul,
   What could they answer was their goal –
For which they bore war's fatal aches?"

– "Let our work rot above our heads
   We sleep secure. Many do less.
   We wear the world in quietness,
And, dumb within our earthen beds,

"Are sign that, against every real
   Interest of earthly happiness,
   And spiritual hope, we did confess
The queer voice of the heart's ideal.

"And if our night of death were less,
   Or for our fight the world less wrong,
   Our testimony would be less strong –
We should have sold our happiness.

"We gave it, as it is, away.
   We prove life's not all simple laws.
   Deep into earth our flesh withdraws.
Our lives have vanished from your day."

THE ASSIGNATION
1916

O Friend! chance bears an equal hand.
   Appointment vague, provisional,
But sure as that entrenched we stand
   I make; and keep it as I shall!

Wait for me, by slow Lethe's stream
   Or lit Valhalla's halls of mirth,
Or in the nightmare land of dream,
   Or lifeless in the sullen earth;

But meet me! prize to shot of mine
   Or sender of the lead I stop!
Bear no ill-will. If fates conjoin
   You winged me with that gun you drop!

Beneath the murmuring hood of night
    Where memory is only fact,
Let us discuss the tears of fight
    With martial courtesy and tact...

Then it's not wrong to fraternise:
    Night can draw in on us no more,
No more ill can our wits devise
    Either for other. There ends war.

THE FIRING PARTY
1917

I shall not see them sweating at that task:
It was too much of any man to ask;
The death that gets you certain, soon or late;
Meanwhile the mess, the mud, the noise, the hate.
But I shall see through bandages the white
Cheeks round the gun-barrel, and then night.
Was it cowardice from fight's short shock to creep
Into a nightmare of eternal sleep;
My only fault that I misjudged my spirit
And volunteered, and now disgrace inherit?
Still will bombardment fill the noisy sky,
Still will old comrades fight and wonder why;
But soon they'll join me – those that I out-raced,
Reaching the goal too early, and disgraced.
The flower of sleep will blow on either grave
And wheat frequent the coward as the brave,
Disliking only where the trenches ploughed
And ordnance delved, and fiery liquids flowed,
Where war's red feet his wicked winepress trod,
An outrage on the peaceful hopes of God.

SMOKE AND DIAMOND

The Pursuit

What deep abyss seen by earth's sky
Will make my flight reality?
You stir beneath a leaf. You soar
On lark-like wings to heaven's door;
You pry and peer at a lighted feast,
Yours the ambition-shattering jest.
You trap in loneliness the soul,
You throw it in pain's burning bowl;
Your stars, high-hung in the flat sky,
Glitter through winds which saunter by
And bring perfumed relief, and sigh.
Yet where the sea outpaces mind,
So wide one might as well be blind,
With a squall blowing up, and bow
Breasting an oily Vee that now
Seems out to the world's end to plough,
You strike men with sky's steady stare
And suddenly surprise them there.
We dare not touch on sea or land
A single thing, or rest or stand
For fear we brush your outstretched hand.
O man's freewill was never meant
To come from one omnipotent,
It makes freewill a jest. Remain
No degradations whose dark stain
You have not worn, and called it gain,
Save one – You wait and falter still
To lead man from temptation till
He does not his but Heaven's will.

Impregnable

I do not feel you near like a girl's cheek
   Flesh against flesh as near as flesh can near
   Laid upon mine, her whispers in my ear.
I don't need that, I do not need to seek
The moon, the hour the occasion for a week
   To marry briefly "mine" and "near" and "dear"

And hustle passion with the step of fear
And then find chains of deathless vowance weak.

You approach me not at all – because you rise
   From jagged, night-blotted caverns of the heart
   To moon it with the tides of spirit's sea.
Though their full term of years the world's rams prise
   They cannot take those gates whose sesame
   Their own lord never heard of from the start.

Reason

I know you're right and I am wrong,
   I know that where I catch you as
Illogical, shows in the long
   Run, who the real illogic has.

But still I cannot see your justice
   And who shall guarantee blind faith?
Then – "since your heart's and reason's lust is
   To accuse God, do it" – my soul saith.

And till the time when I shall hear
   Your explanation face to face
I shall not cease my war through fear –
   Nor shall I give five minutes' grace.

The Double

A little figure, like a young lamb lost
   In February, stares at me
   More sadly tearful, more reproachfully
Than any human should – but he's a ghost.

And through the azure spaces of my youth
   He moved, and for the tiny stains
   The unkind air on him constrains
Holds me responsible and doubts my ruth.

For I am conscious; he was but a light
   In quiet pastures drifting round;
   His baby sins to all my crimes are bound
He thinks: I, mine to his: and which is right?

Predestination

Lord, out of your omniscience you know
   A way to save us and yet keep free will;
But the fine flower of independence only
   Thus flourishes – to think you might have saved,
Might, and did not; wherefore in man's damnation
   We have the answer to your Incarnation.

Ariel

Repeated pain had blurred by wont
   The tortures of your cramping tree,
And then there came at last the spell
   Flesh can't resist, and you were free.

O was it good to feel the clouds
   And the long rollers of the sea
Bearing the body wood once viced,
   While you drink air that was less free?

Or did you, past receding skies
   See freedom widening unconfined
As if to blow the self you know
   Out into chaos deep and blind?

The Song of Songs

The world's tongue scandals sinful fleshly creatures,
    Who plays with pitch
Reaps but a dirty harvest, and the natures
    Of bodies is to itch.

The flying year to England's may-bloom myrtle
    Commutes the snows,
And on the eaves the sleek and dreamy turtle
    Is moaning in a doze.

He came and kissed my burning lips in darkness.
    Past belief
Was the fragrance of his hands, and the starkness
    When he fled, like a thief.

The Chase

I groped up ordinary stairs,
    My hand was on the rail,
When rose unspeakable dark fears
    That froze and turned me pale.

No sound. No murmur. But a thought
    From the brain's dark corners went –
Unhesitatingly you're sought
    By an Omnipotent.

"And one day when the soul's off guard
    The ever-waiting ghost
Will chance the hour and burst the ward,
    And you're forever lost.

The night, to undreamed-of confines
    Was silent as the tomb.
I lit the gas like one who signs
    The warrant of his doom.

Betrayal

All good, fair, sweet, not evil that we see,
O Lord, are parts or attributes of Thee, –
Thou art a lover and a soldier, Lord
But all of either would break heart or sword
Ere act as thou dost; The small leveret
Whose vigour bounced him in the trap we set,
The bloom-bemocking insect which betrays
Beauty-mad butterflies into his maze,
The tender deer, the lamb compared to thee,
Whose lives quick claws bereave in agony,
The peaceful city, built in confidence
On earth's broad breast, gulped to a doom immense,

All these were borne upon thy divine wings
Swam in thy bosom, with thy crown were kings,
When on the very field, while all the air
Shivered to see what wonders the Good dare,
Thou ran'st and left us, conscious friends and those
Unknowingly of thy party – to their foes.

The Question

Wind and rain spell *never again*.
    Autumn speaks of *Death*,
Go slow, go slow, cry rook and crow,
    Patience Sorrow saith......

Now the earth lies dumb as the skies –
    "If separate elements
Speak, Earth, the whole of man's sad soul
    What speaks *thy* voice immense?

God?" I cried – but far and wide
    The leaves blew aimlessly
And field and hill were twice as still
    As the sky-bosomed sea.

The Answer

Lord, if thy lore be infinite, Thou know'st
A way to save us and yet keep freewill,
But none the less (so windingly thou go'st
About thy ways) have it as it is still,
For the fine flower of independence only
Thus flourishes – to think thou mightst have saved
Hell (and the nights wherein we are so lonely
And all insults Time's hand so deep hath graved)
Mightst, but didst not, wherefore in man's damnation
We have an answer to Thy Incarnation.

The Physician

If pain were pain writ bare
    Who'd not invent you?
Its fires, high tragedy, the lovely face of care,
    We only meant you.

And now while from dark eaves
    The earth is drinking,
In sorrow seasonal as these falling leaves
    The soul is sinking.

This is, I hope, the draught
    Your kind hands have prepared,
(For always when too soullessly I laughed
    Next hour, almost, I cared).

Else for all the black nights
    Made bitter with heart's rain
When the pale mists rolling round yellow street-lights
    Exhaust the heart with pain.

For the hours when (as now) in derisions
    Hope crumples away,
For the unending frustration of one's dear ambitions
    What have you that can pay?

The Road

Fair are thy mountains, monarchs of clear streams,
    And dear thy pastures, Lord! dear all the wide
    Rich, ancient, seasonable countryside
Whose fresh air like a bird's throat shakes and sings.

Its thickets creak and cleave and gently sway
    With winged creatures or the pushing fawn
    Whose little lives are all one solid dawn,
Their mental skies encircled by one day.

And only man strange as a road might be
    Whose edges languished with the earth's delight,
    Implacably rushing on through day and night
Over the hills and falling in the sea.

Courage

This is the noblest words man's lips can frame –
    Never to yield.
This is the real and enduring fame
    Of battlefield.

Clouds flee and rocks are broken with the wave
    Against them hurled,
But man need never bow above the grave,
    Not in this world.

When qualities all beautiful and bland
    Desert the soul,
Courage sings like a swan, still with command
    From Pole to Pole.

And this I know more true because the gale
    Now has its way;
But, when it's live or die, I will not bend,
    Or so I say.

The Dialogue

"Soul, why art thou unquiet? Why shake
With winds bitterer than sorrow had?

"Soul, why of sighs thy raptures make
As though thy ideal heaven were sad?

"All through day's weary, weary light
You sigh and sicken. Are you tired?"

"You through the long turning night
Ache and throb too; and I am tired!"

Spring Thoughts

Say he returns – the swallow wheels
    Back in the van of spring –
Returns but *Go again*. Birth seals
    The death of anything.

Weary the pilgrimage: the fight
   To other times and spheres
Lifted perhaps; and burning light
   May eat away our fears.

But stubborn through a million springs,
   The swallow at our mast,
We'll drive, until the echo rings
   The Spring is here to last.

A spring which will not pass away;
   A bird whose wings are bound,
A dawn which prows eternal day,
   A bliss calm and profound.

The Search

I sought him in the sinless skies,
   And in the drama of the years.
The long lands where the lone rock cries
   Gave voice to secret fears.
I stared my own soul in the eyes.

I looked into the crystal's heart,
   The dark and twisted world of space
Swung its eccentric planes apart,
   But in that haunted place
There's nothing satisfies my smart.

Like snowflakes human bodies fled:
   They rose in patterns rich and rare:
Round swept the living and the dead
   Borne upon empty air –
As vain a pageant as the Preacher said.

So I at last admit the springs
   Chatter their inmost hearts right out
And that the world of science brings
   Its final end about:
And that mankind are their own kings;

And call that *Where*? the God I seek;
    Take it as a testimony
That still a mansion for the weak,
    A fastness for the free,
Beds not Procrustean for the freak

Are gained through chinks that are not there,
    Within a God for Whom's no room,
Because naught answers that same *Where*
    Men ask unto the tomb
And then dissolve in empty air.

Matter

Each day, foursquare, before my window
    This solid house
With dark, with cold inveterate calm
    Stares through the boughs.

But whether sunlight sidles fair
    Or on its face
The evening droops; I know it shares
    None of that grace.

I know that still, within its dark
    Its secret heart
Sits its unchanging element,
    A thing apart,

And Love and Hope, those fays of air,
    Mere wind-borne bubbles,
Dance, showing through and through the hues
    Of joys or troubles –

More answerable than my flesh,
    They bow, and bend,
And shoot with living colour; yet
    They burst; they end.

Thou only, God, hast learnt the art
    To change and stick,
Support the superincumbent flesh
    And yet be quick.

Thy face to me more changeful is
    Than the sky's veils,
And yet, at last, upon thy heart
    Time's vigour fails.

Complexity

This soul of mine, for all its scurrying thoughts,
    Deep-diving memory, and yawing will,
Is but a child's simplicity of noughts
    By body's babel – even when it's still.

Mechanic sinews, living bone, pleached nerves,
    Republic by some rare refinement knit
Into a sudden clap of shimmering curves
    A moment – then earth drinks up all of it.

And "I" – a breath, a name spiritualised,
    Without this engine unknown to mankind,
A trembling smoke, sailor unadvised
    What start, what bourne, what route, and whence the wind.

Rise, breath, and body fall! God has no parts,
    That homogeneous and eternal O
Whatever devolution waits our hearts
    This woven world has brought sufficient woe.

The Device

I slept and dreamed. The demiurge
    Was tinkering with the human soul,
And all life's labyrinthine surge
    He watched, and saw it whole.

The soul lagged – like a symphony
    It hung in space but could not sound.
God made a small adjustment; she
    Dropped, music, to the ground.

Smooth man sang to the sphere's slick dreams,
    A mathematic luxury –

But what's to God solution seems
    Quite otherwise to me.

It crusts the night with chymic flowers,
    One fears to handle honest flesh;
It has entrapped my midnight hours
    In a metallic mesh,

Transformed the day to Light's harsh stare;
    And made the balm of summer vex;
Loved – wasted; used – choked; feared – a snare;
    In God's mechanics – Sex.

Smoke and Diamond

Smoke tells me my eternal livelihood
    Is not in breath blown like the Wandering Jew
    About the regions of the world it knew,
Finding desolate what it once thought good.

Nor shall I pass to caverns of the night
    Concealed in sunlit mountains of the day;
    But to a tenement more real than they
Withdraw, into the inmost heart of Light. –

So says the diamond, whose candour lives
    Its four dimensions almost to their full,
    Scorning complexity that makes life null
And the spirituality short duration gives.

The smoke still rises from the steaming sod,
    Spirit of earth more material than matter.
    I shall sink through this life whose smoke soars but to flatter,
And drop into the bosom of my God.

More Proverbs

The man who says he fears to die
His whole life's purpose doth deny.
They make themselves God's laughing-stock
Who at Death's portals wildly knock.

Who to paint heaven undertook
Through his own body tried to look

The man who's smoothed the path of love
Has made himself beloved above.
He who refraineth from the flesh
Much helps or hinders heaven's wish.
That man has lived without a heart
Who must make choice 'twixt love and art.

The saint's humility doth tell
The world's a lie built over hell,
And that the route to Paradise
Is circular to mortal eyes.
Let not soul's solitude distress,
For the soul's made of loneliness.
The glittering stars forever sing,
Dead is the unremembering thing,
And every glory vainly glows
In him who's greater than he knows.

If a Good God's omnipotent
Why was such power to Evil lent?
If evil is the lack of good,
God's power is not withstood.
If the devil invented evil
Who invented then the devil?
If good and ill earth's kingdom sever,
How can the struggle finish ever?
Who in heaven would rest him quiet
When those he loves hell's furies diet?

Round his own centre he revolves,
Not life's, who all these doubts resolves.
Not stars, compass, dead-reckoning guide
Life's mariner, but life's own tide.
Life is a story, not a scheme,
Not Satan's reasons, but God's dream.
Ask not if mind or matter's real,
All is reality you feel.
Be not afraid, let out your sail,
Life's winds fail not, you cannot fail.
Powers that can your ship direct
Will guide you even when it's wreckt.

Point of Departure
1928-1936

POET'S INVOCATION

Teach me first to forget all ways of speech,
Languages, phrases, words, tricks, prettinesses.
Teach me to speak.

Who teach? Apollo? Or the Holy Ghost?
Δαιμον? No, something stubborn in the blood.
Then, learn to speak.

Of what? Love? Courage to endure? Or age?
Or sitting in the sun? No, of oneself.
Then speak.

To whom? The next-door neighbouring man?
One's friends? Posterity? No, to oneself.
Then

POLAR EXPEDITION

Sublime extremes, round which the earth rotates!
Unclaimed, unsovereignable barren states!
Where rarely mankind visits, and in vain
To challenge the great whale's untroubled reign,
Or flout the lonely bird which never sings
But like a snowflake with the blizzard wings,
Or rests unmoving, flock on flock on flock,
With bended head, part of the living rock.

   But some have penetrated, and apart
They walk, the icy secret in their heart,
Escaped with bitten fingers from that vale
Of endless ice, to tell their stubborn tale.

   These say, that at the barren ruthless Pole
The mortal floats, as if within a bowl,
Around whose rim days circularly run
Sucking down in their molten race the sun.
God help the man who first endured that trial,
For whom at dawn evaded his espial,

Light and the sun – still o'er the wastes of snow
Lay darkness revelling in their overthrow....

   In torrid zones the ardent sap is rising,
Mounting the sky, strong in its sure surmising,
But towards the Pole the frightened venturers steal,
And as they move their hands go out to feel –
Their fingers are their eyes, and darkness stays
Sullenly lingering endless days and days.
The bear goes padding by on furry sole,
The sleek shy seal retreats from the dark Pole,
The liquid sun flows round this island night
But far within, forgotten of the light,
These men are buried; each in his tent stays,
In his boat of light voyaging the blind days,
Each with a steady flame to guard and cherish,
For light is life and in the dark they perish;
And only the empty round of need and sleep
Marks their vain passage on the obscure deep.
And lo! when the day dawns and the sun swims,
Above the black horizon redly skims,
Each with the same enquiry stares at each,
In sudden inquisition scant of speech,
And each stares back, seeking with eyes that glow,
The change that peers from every face they know,
Out of the mask-like cheeks, white as the Polar snow!

   As clear as truth is the cold ambient air,
Across whole continents voyagers stare,
Or in the sudden fog horizons go
And drowned they walk beneath a sea of snow.
The ocean floor slopes downward; in the sky
The false horizon floats to lure their eye.

   O many the wanderer sees a haven clear,
In seeming but a scant day's journey near,
And when, fatigued, they pitch their tent and sleep,
Still swims the landmark far out on the deep,
And as they follow across seas of snow
Still keeps aloof however far they go.
And sense-distracting things that are not there
Hang silently in the thin guileless air,
Standing the scrutiny of eye and glass

They loom, and then as airily they pass –
Trees, harbours, tents of co-exploring souls
Daring the secret malice of the Poles.

   Yet still horizons lure their spirits on,
Past endless snow still must their goal be won.
The ceaseless purity should blind their eyes,
But these they veil, ignore the misty skies,
And press still onward. The horizon goes,
And vision falters in the sea of snows.
Well, let dead-reckoning guide them – and the stars;
No rock, no life the eternal whiteness mars,
Their track runs out behind, across the snow,
Or on? – for now one cannot certainly know,
But there, where recognition fails they find
A spiritual location of the mind,
An end, a goal, which finding, they forget
The death, disaster, hunger, toil and sweat.

   Yet they are lovely, are these icy shores,
When spring flings out her treasure on their floors:
The flowers blow as in more florid lands,
The reindeer and the musk-ox browsing stands,
The youngling by his loving mother nursed,
Bold arctic kine that brave the Polar worst,
And moths and flies weave in the champagne air –
Their little lives and nimble wings will dare
The great Pole's dumb and icy sullenness,
And farther North their airy legions press.

   Amazed, entranced, the first that ventured nigh,
Saw a vague whiteness fill the Northern sky.
The ship's bluff forefoot entered cumbered seas
Through the thin ice she ploughed, sped by the breeze,
And see! as on they press, bloom flowers of ice,
The tiny spikes in intricate device.

   And see! the Icebergs, proud queens of the Pole,
Who sweep the seas and own no wind's control.
Steadily on through floe and pack they sweep,
And as they move a gentle rocking keep.

    Proud mountains! you are doomed at last to fall!
The warmer waters batter on your wall.
On, on you press, now sailing brighter seas
But these so fair, are fatal territories
Decay will reach up to your steel-blue crown
And all your sheering vastness topple down.
Meanwhile you lord it, patiently aloof.
Among the justling floes your snowy roof
Upreaches as a musing hero moves
Among the crowd, busy with hates and loves –
Thought-wrapt, with conscious purpose passing still
His destiny and greatness to fulfil.....

    As men, so brutes within the awful cold
Life's brief tenure momentarily hold –
Poor plants obsessed by the great natural need –
For four long months the vegetations feed
And for four months lie tranced in Arctic night
– A living death ruled by the dearth of light.
But the cold quickens the whale's savage heart,
Their ravening heads attempt the floes to part,
The sleek-eyed seals, all graceful oiliness,
Urge over the thin floes in mad distress,
But the whale furious for the living food,
Dyes all the water with their piteous blood.
A race apart, than men more kind and wise,
The penguins walk, with speculating eyes;
In the wide silence of the glassy Pole
Which awes and terrifies the human soul,
They in their millions scan the league of snow,
And see in it the country that they know....

    Why has the scene – the ice as still as death –
The clear blue outlines undimmed by fog's breath –
The lonely icebergs locked in solemn thought –
Why does it hold their senses so ensnared,
That all these perils, though well-known, are dared?

    The Isles of Spice first lured their stretching mind,
But still the North-West way they could not find,
And yet they came – like icebergs moved by deep
Currents of thought, beyond air's power to keep.

O, all man's life is but a barren Pole:
The icebergs move within the human soul,
The explorer strives to reach the desired mark,
In the long silence of an Arctic dark,
And if he reach the mark, or always fail,
Still drop he must, within death's chilling vale,
Clutched by the roving frostbite death, locked tight
In the unrelenting ice of the Pole's night.

POEM

High on a bough beneath the moonlight pale
That over-rated bird the nightingale
Sang and sang on. I thought my heart would break
At first, to feel again that forlorn ache
Across the waste of history – "Wine, Red Wine!"
Fitzgerald's Nightingale, with voice divine,
Called out – "to stain my rose-love's pale cheeks red!"
And Keats arose, among the wintry dead,
And testifies, his sunken eyes ashine –
The song; dusk; dream; and oozy eglantine!

But these are dead and dumb. This is a fowl
Hatched from an ordinary egg. The owl
Like generation owneth. The world wags
And from a pure tropism the small bird brags,
His vocal cords to something in the air
Reacting, never of the spring aware,
While still more passive, dumb and deaf and blind
Keats and Fitzgerald slumber, clay-confined;
Close-hugged by greedy earth, whose barren vales
Nurse for one Keats a billion nightingales.

THE DIALECTIC
A SESTINA

A. She is my arms' delight, a spanking beauty
Puffed out with all the easy gauds of body;
The wood-man owns himself her docile subject;

Her gorgeous blood is a delirious spirit
Compact of some refined celestial matter
For which the charge of breathing is no object.

B.   In reason's sight she is a common object,
Oppressed with gravity like any body;
For wit a butt, for algebra a subject;
I cannot find in her a trace of spirit
Or aught diverse from any other matter,
To which an S ascribes the P of beauty.

A.   She is a heavenly Form derived from Beauty,
Shed in pure passion by that Holy Spirit
In contemplation of its timeless object.
Space is her nurse; the womb of fiery matter
Engendering from Delight her perfect body
By pure conception of its divine subject.

B.   She is to death and age and sickness subject,
The common harriers of everybody:
To ripe; to rot; these are the things that matter;
The roses blow and fall, so blows, falls, Beauty.
The ardent flesh is but a sorry object,
A pinch of ice will make it lose its spirit.

A.   I love her in her thoughts, a gracious spirit
That wanders mothlike through the flowers of beauty;
Cerberus to her light passage cannot object
And Rhadamanthos from some weighty matter
Looks up, and smiles; Hell's king to her is subject
And thinks his fairest shade her simple body.

B.   You will find all your hell in that dear body,
Once taste the poison of her painted beauty!
In lust's soft dreams desire's delightful object;
In flesh disgusting, it is sweet in spirit,
For you will find desire a slavish subject
But being given mastery, no such matter.

A.   She will atone for the distress of matter
And sullen obstinacy of the brute body;
She gives a certain glow to every subject
And lights life's unconvincing flux with beauty.

The crass world owes her all it has of spirit.
Before she lived, she was the world's sole object.

B.   She is a lie like any other object;
You cannot know her more than any body.
Around her going some transient patch of spirit
Your eye projects; and language calls it beauty,
Betrayed by errors to which words are subject
Like all the gross secretions of pure matter.

A.   What though I am betrayed, what does it matter?
A hundred lovers may have had her body,
But for an hour, to my desire a subject.
We dallied in the inmost caves of beauty;
Our pleasure then was a sufficient object;
We did not weight it with the cares of spirit.

B.   You mean you drank her as you might drink spirit?
Only the fanatic to this would object,
But you are you and also you are body:
The weakened back; the coarsening of her beauty;
The idiocy; the pox; sores running matter:
I'll not pursue more an unpleasant subject.

A.   Of Shakespeare's songs she is the well-known subject:
He knew the quirks and twistings of her spirit;
Of young Catullus' verse appropriate object;
For nightingale, I claim, the worthy matter;
Say but her name, you have named every beauty;
She is of all men's dreams the perfect body.

B.   Of your defeat she is the living body;
Your stifled bitternesses make her matter;
Your green ambition, turned from its true object,
By some glove-like inversion of the spirit
Has found her vulgar bosom fitting subject
Of all you looked, longed, thought, desired of beauty.

A.   No other beauty want I than her body.
B.   You will be subject to unworthy object.
A.   Her spirit glows
                    B.   Like any corrupt matter.

THE APOSTATE

All cunning freaks that try hard to convert us
To humpbackdom or to a cloven lip,
One-eyed things, slime dripping from their ears,
Joined at the navel, with protrusive warts –

There is an odd conviction in their ways.
They wear as well as us, and shuffle on
Certain of some last entrance into heaven
Where angel hands will stroke their horned snouts.

Let us live piously and love our neighbours;
Let us live prettily and oil our hair;
Let us live gracefully and dance like waves.
We know the rubric and we play the game.

"Framed from our birth proficient in disgust,"
They answer, "We ignore your inbred musts.
We have a way of shuffling that suffices.
Secrete; excrete; remember. Needs there more?

"You are very snug and moral as you flaunt
On sun-tanned flanks the rags of righteousness.
He warned in case your own conventions rot you,
Puffed up because your Christ had all ten toes.

"The body bears a cancer in its womb.
Can you hear us club-foots scuttling in your attics?
Or feel your clean skin mottling into shark-skin?
And a jump in the graph of monstrous births?"

THE REQUEST

Let some tough fibre in my being win
Even though it pulls the flesh awry; ruckles it
Like a botched shoe.

When all is done, it's not the airs and graces
Time's acid spares, but a defiant coarseness
In the grain.

And men call courage what is obstinacy:
A sulky habit holding to the trail
When it is silly.

It is not courage – or staunch-heartedness –
But the wrecked spirit's bias, a lump of metal
In the wood's belly.

THE CONSOLATIONS OF RELIGION

In the long breathing spaces of Creation,
Stroking his ancient beard, God meditates
Diverse elaborate tortures for the men
Who thwart the progress of his great Idea –
Protracted roastings, livers vulture-torn,
White solitudes of cataleptic swoon,
Vertiginous rotation on great wheels...
God smiles and one of the obsequious angels
Pours a new plague upon our stiff-neckt race.

We too, retaining in life's dissolution
God's ill-advised concession of free-will
Awarded in a moment of distraction,
Devise delightful fancies of the Deity
Bored past endurance by His omnipresence,
Omnisciently surveying His defects
Or frying like a sausage in a bonfire,
His love's unquenchable infinity.

THE UNSPEAKABLES

We have no secrets. Nothing we can't show.
This century has slipped its breeches off.
Even the sacrament of love is unreserved.

Nothing will come of nothing. Change your mind.

We have no minds; only a local glow
Left by the passage of the frigid worm
That willynilly traverses spacetime.

Have you no signs or wonders in your bodies?

Moore's bosom smelt of violets. Alexander
Relieved him of rose-water, we of money.
It is pure gold. Do what you like with it.

What of the various gods with saving power?

We know those autoerotisms too well.
The soul is saved (and damned) by copulation.
The soul is feminine. She is a bitch.

I have found consolation in great art.

One does indeed. It is a great relief
When some imaginary Grecian bares
His marble skin, or Shakespeare finds the purse
In which the liquid gold of dream is hidden.

You too must die! Have you rehearsed your death?

Good gracious, no. The doctors are at work
And the State hides all sharp-edged instruments.
There is a well-known fondness in the soul
For self-destruction which will pull it through.

That way lies madness so near to great wit.

Nonsense! We gratify our least desire;
We rub our little bellies with delight;
You will expire the day your stifled guts
Explode into your brains; we shall break wind.

Have you no ideals? Why was Plato born?

We have an undigested residue
That our rebellious bowels will not pass.
We must confess we do know what you mean.

THE DANGER

Beware of virtue, said my nurse to me
And shun the Good. Keep your tender shins
Away from Truth.

I had forgotten, and the potent acid
Of your truth-loving soul has cracked my talent,
Colourful, flawed.

For my feet slipped, distracted by your call,
Seeing you in the open heights, deep miles
Past my climb's goal.

You are no fit companion for my ways.
You have debauched, seduced me into virtues
Where I shall drown.

THE WEAKNESS

Past many a tempest trying to the heart's temper;
By many a blowing whale with bulgy brow;
Caught on a leeshore – yet in the outcome living –
I hope to harbour.

Do not confuse my hopes with hopes of heaven.
The mud is rank; port dues exorbitant;
The urchins steal my dinghy. Yet the place
Is what it is.

The soft swan rears it on the silent river;
The dolphin droops below the dabbled swell.
Here I careen and do my ship's last service,
And die in bed.

THE NATURE OF THE PHYSICAL WORLD

I found myself sitting in the attic with Time, an old man
Counting his treasures over;
His feathers were battered and dusty; he was tired,
And I was tired.

"The Universe is as empty as a squeezed orange," he said.
"There is nothing much left
Except trinkets, and one or two bundles of letters.
My brains are a little dusty," he said.
"And mathematicians scuttle among them like mice
And I am tired of the bumpkins who keep on digging in the
            allotment of Space."

Time kept on sorting his rubbish with shaking hands
And I helped him turn over the knick-knacks;
One, I confess, appealed to me –
An affair of gold, very curiously wrought, in the likeness of a bird
With small bright ruby eyes.
"That nightingale!" cried Time. With trembling fingers
He wound it up. "And now a song," he said
"For old Time's sake!"

>   "Death shall not triumph over hope
>   Though night snows its raucous aggrandise;
>   Summer across the mountain posts
>   (And) throws back error in death's eyes
>
>   "And though at night the horizon flares
>   And sunlight in sea's embrace drowns
>   Like a young phoenix from its byre
>   Day will return with extra crowns."

"I am bored," said Time, throwing it out of the window,
"And yet it has the air of a poet I used to love.
These trinkets are out of fashion now.
Even the sun has a beastly bourgeois air.

I am frankly sick of my business
And feel it unfair I am kept so close to my work.
But the Master is ageing too – that ripe invention
Which charmed us so in his youth has ceased to function,

And the worst of it is, the audience is out of control.
They are wandering round the stage behind the scenes,
Prodding the dusty backs of drops with their umbrellas,
Prying into the engine from which the god descends.
That's the end, and in my view –
And I've been stage-manager here since the beginning –
They might as well walk out and close the box-office."
And he slammed the lid of his trunk with a spiteful bang;
While far away, down on the pavement, I heard
The click of clockwork and a throaty song
As urchin fingers found the nightingale.

THE LAST JUDGMENT

I was present in the Press-box at the Judgment.
When the heavens fell down like cracked plaster
And the Judge, on a dais of red velvet
Disposed of the resurrected souls.

One man came forward with a peacock
And, plucking off the great tail feathers,
Proffered God the bare rump of the bird.

But the black-coated company of angels
Carolled: "Blessed,
Blessed be the face of truth!"

Then a woman came forward, a widow
And with a gesture I thought unseemly
Exposed her bosom and thighs.

But the stiff-shirted company of angels
Chanted: "Blessed,
Blessed be the name of love."

Then I (it was most unprofessional)
I opened my mouth to speak
But what with my pride and terror
Instead of speech I hiccoughed.

77

But the bald-headed company of angels
Cried: "Blessed,
Blessed be the voice of the bard!"

And now we are living in Heaven,
We three, the virtuous sheep
And, my arm on Heaven's bar resting
I lean over and gaze in the gulf

Whence our nostrils are soothed by the odour
Acrid, of nightingale burning
Or a rose decomposing in smoke.

THE SURVIVAL

Shall I preserve intact the fine facade
Or let it crumble, not with age or illness
Or weight of metal, but merely from fatigue?

I have raised and kept it upright with some pain
And got no credit for it. Well, the effort
Increases with the years. Then let it drop!

But can I? Do I really lurk behind there
Scratching, or worse, like a bare-buttocked mandril,
Or do *I* embody the sculpturesque aloofness

The mellow generosity of swags,
Marble and undercut, of balanced windows,
Of Roman gravity and long arcades?

I wonder now. And less and less I feel
Myself gesturing lewdly in dark and private
And more in public, calm, impressive, solid.

Hollow – agreed! A sham – let me confess it!
But still, supposing I permit myself
My once-so-frequent wish to let go all

And find I have become the fine facade,
And so must vanish in a puff of dust –
Self-monumental cairn of sculptured fragments?

I feel a certain sympathy for plaster.
There is instructive virtue in a pose
Which pays its smirking homage to the Real.

THE TRADITION

Poets unborn will sing of this
Teasing the larynx into thread
Keats upon Shakespeare's shoulders climbs
At the new burden with a groan
Seneca's bald pate sinks in bog
Poets unborn will sing of this
And from discordant echoes try
To pick distinct a twinkling tune
Hark the grey-whiskered dragon chases
St. George to darker caves of dream
Where lair our starving pale-eyed bogeys
Poets unborn will sing of this
And in the savage infant's game
Smith puts his hand on Brown's on Smith's
On Brown's on Smith's on Brown's on Smith's
And starting up – the nightingale!
Each lays a finger on his lips
But with a whirr the music ends
The broadcast of a record of
A record of a broadcast of
Some documented vertebrate
Whose stuffed heart moulders in a case
Poets unborn will sing of this
And vex the reed-grown breast of Time
Whose crop secretes a pigeon's milk
Of pre-digested nutriment
Our nerves will lose their sinewy pith
The common man from such a diet
Will turn away the action flexing

Huge muscles in his golden skin
We beat our spare breasts in contempt
Poets unborn will sing of this.

TO –

I read your poems. I have a vile trick
Of sucking grass stems for the sweetish pulp.
It soothes the nerves. You know I do not smoke?
To-day the soothing ritual performed,
I got a sudden tickling in my throat –
A seed lodged in the larynx. I have coughed
But still the tickling makes my weak eyes weep,
A dull discomfort at the back of thought.
How did you get that trick of writing verse?
Mine melt upon the palate without pain,
As bland as the post-prandial cigarette,
As null. No reader has coughed blood for me....

CLASSIC ENCOUNTER

Arrived upon the fields of asphodel
I strolled towards the military quarters
To find the sunstruck shades of Allied soldiers
Killed on the Chersonese.

I met a band of weary palefaced men
Attired in strange accoutrements. It seemed
That I had lost my way. "Where did you fall?
Not at Gallipoli!"

And one – the leader, with a voice of gold –
answered me. "No, a deep disgrace was ours.
We are Athenian hoplites who sat down
Before young Syracuse.

"Need I recount our too notorious end?
The hesitancy of our General Staff,
The battle in the harbour, when Hope fled
And we were smitten?"

"But why disgrace?" I asked. "For many men
(As your Nicias said, the eloquent fool)
Have done the cruel things men will, and then
Borne what men must."

"Not our disgrace in that," the soldier said,
"But we are those proficient in the arts,
Freed in return for the repeated verses
Of our Euripides.

"Those honeyed words did not soothe Cerberus"
(The leader smiled) "To Charon seemed not hire
Sufficient, nor with Rhadamanthos ranked
As mitigation.

"Only with men, born victims of their ears,
The chorus of the tearful Troades
Prevailed to gain the freedom of our limbs
And waft us back to Athens.

"In this abode of military men
We wander without peers, not fallen nor
Survivors in a military sense,
Hence the disgrace."

He turned, and as the rank mists took them in
They chanted of the God to whom men pray
Whether he be Compulsion, or All-Fathering,
Or Fate and blind.

THEY SAID

"Not capable,
Impotent,
Past it now."
Grumbling and snuffling

Old grey-beard goes
Up the stairs.
His bones cold;
Hand on the rail
Gives a great roar,
Sees the white
Upturned faces,
And with a guffaw
Stamps to bed.
"Not so old.
We can
Show 'em all yet."

So my technique
Lacking the clear
Patient spirit,
Lacking the strong
Biting wit,
Lacking the mellow
Opulence...

In its day
Living high,
Lovely ladies,
Wine and singing
Came its way,
Riding on
With thundering hooves.
Now it totters
In loose clothes,
Shrunken, old.
The shout's the same.

THE VISITOR

The roads are full of soldier ghosts to-day –
Armistice Day, a memorable day in town,
When the puffy generals sweep through the silent streets,
When the bugles wail in the sleeping ear of God,
When the mothers weep, and the soldiers march like angels,
And the flags flutter, proud thoughts in the mourning breasts.

I poked a likely lad in the bony ribs.
"Hey, lad!" I said. "You were buried years ago.
Why do you tramp, tramp, clatter through our streets?
You are rotten and walking. The thousands of us who die
At the wheels of the atrocious motoring hun
At least have the taste to moulder peaceably.
Why are you up and abroad, O likely lad?"

And he answered gruffly. "I must play the game
As I was taught to do, a likely lad.
I wish I were back in the safe and stuffy grave,
Dicing for mole-skins with old knuckle-bones
Or swapping yarns with my sergeant – a splendid man.
But I must turn out in the chilling dawn of Time
And face the biting breezes of this earth.
The generals are massing at the Cenotaph,
The Sovereign is honouring us with poppy-wreaths:
I must play the game; I must act in a soldierly manner."

THE OBJECT

Mortal I am as a man, winning the world to my ways.
Immortal I am as an image, a piece of the splendid past,
A monument of myself, an accident in time's amber.

Stopped are my stone senses to life's elusive fragrance
For ever refreshed in savour – or liker a leaping flame
Spreading in ceaseless disorder, consuming the cause of its colour.

Eyed like those ice-bound fishes that, as we skate swiftly over
Stare at our sliding soles – out of the tide of time,
Parted by a clear pane, seen yet separate,
I shall lie at last in the dark ditch of death.

THE SECRET

I will not strive to win
Your body to touch, to waken
With these hot hands the flesh
Imagined well enough
Night and day.

I will disdain to move
To gleams of appetite
Your mind, that might be swayed
By the effect of speech
Such as this.

I will wholly delete
From the world's polite stare
Evidence of any love
Beyond the veiled witness
Of this song.

I will forbid my heart
To entertain at night
Dreams that might compromise
The wandering phantasmata
Of our souls.

I will conceal in fact
From you and everyone
The nature of the act
That now I solemnly
Here renounce.

And lastly I propose
By a misuse of will
To hide from my own mind
My want, and with this song
End the matter.

THE AUDIENCE

Here in my armchair from the world's work resting
I sit, and spare brief audience. *Hear our prayer!*
Incline thine ear! So beg the various gods
My suitors, devoutly thronging in the hall.

I always had a taste for pantomime
And these dark forces of fertility
Shake an imposing phallus; but they've paled
To spectacled neo-Malthusian gods
Who sourly lurk in ante-natal clinics
Bussing the nurses, as the great God Puck
Now condescends to nip the dairymaids.

Nuzzling my palm I feel the hairy whiskers
Of Yahweh, that Old Man of the apeherd
Sunk into senile quadrupedestrianism,
No longer jealous, doggily prepared
To jostle at the trough with Baal and Jesus.

And Christ? Of course. But anxious to explain
The formal nature of his conjuring tricks
And his contempt for Churches. "All a racket.
They scoop the cash and credit. God gets none."

Buddha and Mahomet have left a note
Apologetically on the salver.
"Our duty to you, Sir. We cannot wait.
Home Office has enforced our deportation.
The unemployment among local gods
English or naturalised...You understand..."

And this poor puling baby with red cheeks
Whom all the others tweak unmercifully
Until he howls with temper? "I'm the State, Sir!"
"James, fetch our tongs and throw this symbol out."

But still, a God there must be; or why work
Without some pet of this kind to come home to?
Oneself? A furtive sideglance in the mirror
Explodes the notion. Or the human race?
An overpowering stench of hot mansbodies
Wafted under the door, explodes that too.

The Gods go one by one and leave me lonely.
The stars of heaven nudge each other, snigger,
And go about their business. I remain
And hear the fire of youth sink in the grate,
New tenants cachinnating on the doorstep,
Rats in the loft, and from the family vaults
Ancestral voices prophesying trouble.

THE KINGDOM OF HEAVEN

I walked down a long, tiled corridor.
There were notices on the walls.
WHITE TIES PLEASE. NO NIGGERS. PLAY THE GAME.
DO NOT SPIT.

THIS WAY TO THE KINGDOM OF HEAVEN.

I went down the long tiled corridor
And at the end someone clattered lift gates.

GOING UP!

I preferred to walk and went up the stairs.

I rapped on the office door and asked for God.
The manager was bald and apologetic.
The manager told me God was out.

I walked back down the stairs, down the corridor.
There are offices it seems across the way.
He may be in there.

PLEASE USE THE SUBWAY.

I used the subway. I am still walking.
I have met many of my friends. Some of them are dead.
The place is well-organised. The commissionaires
Are civil, and put their harps aside
When one speaks to them.

Once there were animals here; insects even;
But they grew tired. They went out to play.
The curiosity of men seems endless.

Even I am too curious to blow my brains out.
I will go on walking although I know it is useless –
I heard the manager muttering in his sleep.

"If they find God the place will have to close.
That is why I tell them God is only Out.
Don't tell the boys God'll never be In."

AGAMEMNON AND THE POET

(Always it's just past the next hill,
   To be reached early in next year)
I press with longing on until
   That hour when I no more shall hear

The nightingales, but be their lips
   And shriek and swing among the trees,
And be the body's flesh that slips
   Round the red bath with loosened knees.

THE ECSTASY

Once I thought I'd found fulfilment here –
A spacious age stretching along the hair
Which parts a point and point of Time.
It seemed I gazed from where stars teem
And saw Earth lying cold and pale;
Within each city's fretted pile
Men fixed as in Death's calm pose
I heard no steps in the streets pass
But all in these, and house, and hall
Were frozen, ecstatic hair to heel.
Each swallow held its arch of grace;

The falling leaf kissed not the grass;
A waterfall was frigid fire.
O marble moment strictly fair!
Soul no more wore life a dim gloss
But steeped, transparent as pure glass
Her rich thoughts patterned in hard lace.
Low hung the brows of the calm heaven
Where the boat swam in the haven,
Tranced with sideways pointing mast
While spray climbed like stony mist.
So still the cold Earth upward stared
Sculpturally aloof, unstirred,
Unseeing...

FIVE TRANSLATIONS FROM THE CHINESE

1

My shadow danced beside me while I climbed
The mountainside, my friend,
To pass with you this last of afternoons.

Farewell! I turned. In front of me
My shadow lay.

2

This fallen tree and in the evening's rain
The dead leaves flying....
This rouses expectation in my mind –
Have I not an appointment here?

Not now. One autumn, beside such a pine
You met her in the rain.

But that was twenty years ago.

3

The wild geese cried above the bamboo leaves
And from the temple on the mountainside
Loud gongs were beaten,
The river murmured in the reeds all night:
And here my boat was moored.

4

A thousand times this precipice I climbed
And, gazing out to sea,
I sought the sail that brought my lover home.
A thousand sails were vain
But one at last wafted my lover back
To lay him with his honoured ancestors.

5

The leaves had fallen from the trees,
There was no moon to light our steps,
And it was long since in the rounded bowl
The wine had laughed at me,
But I was young.

FROM THE GREEK ANTHOLOGY

The world-famed woman sleeps beneath this stone
Who loosed her girdle to one man alone.

FROM THE SAME

Here I, Timocreon, at length did wander
After much food and drink and slander.

ON A SUCCESSFUL PUBLICAN

What spite! Because a coronet
  On all T's goods the user charms
Men call him parvenu – who yet
  Began life with The Royal Arms.

THOUGHT

While gazing at Colonel X

How true this scientific thought I find –
We have *descended* from the monkey kind.

ON A TORY M.P.

This man so truly loved the populace
He hardly ever let them see his face.

IN A CHART ROOM

Being a parallel to a well-known epigram

So many clocks and compasses,
So many charts in black and white –
When all the captain needs to know,
Is just the art of steering right!

EPIGRAM

*Scrawled beneath a nude in the collection of
Sir P--- C---, K.C.*

Be not surprised that I have nothing on.
I am the litigant who always won.

ON A BARRISTER

Say not, O scoffer, that for sordid pence
  The lawyer gets the wrongdoer off whole,
For this man never by his arguments,
  Throughout his life, once saved a guilty soul.

ON THE SAME

On Juris, stranger, salt tears shed –
  He was the Bar's chief prop,
When suddenly he fell down dead.
  (The Barmaid saw him drop.)

ON AN EMPLOYER OF NATIVE CHILD LABOUR

Since but for him they would not have had work,
  A thousand babes supported are by *Burke*.

ON A WICKED MAN

When P – at last to Hades came,
  All gave a welcome shout.
He rushed in through the doors of flame,
  The Devil staggered out.

SALES PASTORAL

On hill and brae the throstle tunes his notes
For Nature's new campaign is now in swing.
Her green buds advertise the latest spring
With propaganda from a thousand throats.

The sales-resistance of our blood succumbs
To copy ever-old yet always new
And when we see the wrapper of sky-blue
We rip the carton up with eager thumbs.

And no consumer yet has ever failed
To clip the coupon promising romance
And leave to Fate the sample's provenance.
Alas, the dismal specimens she has mailed!

Yet business booms beneath self-coloured skies
For sex-appeal is certain not to miss
The contacts first established with a kiss.
Sex has its objects too. Its sweets premise

Establishment of homes in which to live,
Of nests, of dens, to which comes in due course
With the precision of a natural force
The life-assurance representative.

Thus Nature, Being's Arch-executive
Observes the sales-graph of our area leap,
The shearing of the always-patient sheep,
The murmur of the ever-busy hive…

Poor flies that frolic idly in the sun!
Depression lowers above your careless heads
Seen when the sullen sky its anger sheds
And the snow flutters from a heaven of dun.

Seen then too late! The goods are bought, consumed;
The wretched stag roams unemployed, depressed;
The robin, in its summer finery dressed,
Hops out-of-date, to the dole's pittance doomed.

And Nature, looking on her garnered sheaves
Winds up the business that has paid her well.
Her files, her records, scatters she pell-mell
And all the air is filled with flying leaves!

THE VIGIL OF VENUS

Through the woods and through the meadows crowned with may
    old Herrick goes,
Foots it neatly round the woodbine with his paunch and greying
    hair,
Underneath the spreading oaktree, underneath the drooping
    rose
Round he twirls and we have followed, and the agile, and the
    fair.

For to-morrow feast we Venus, Re-creator of the earth,
While the cupids shout and tumble, fly and float above the flowers,
And the larks in loving-kindness praise the prodigies of birth,
And the woodland flings its hair free underneath the nuptial
    showers

She it is who nurses dumbly each within its shining shell
All the rosy blossom-virgins, destined brides of the bright air,
She it is who bids them kindle, with the genial torrents swell,
Burst and blossom, *Io Hymen!* loveliest of the garden's fair.

She it is the crowded ocean, she it is each finny thing
Knows and worships, from whose bosom, woven of the salt and
    wet,
Woven by the ebb and tossing, blows the gossamer of spring,
Catching god and maid and hero in the same delicious net.

Lo, she cometh! and the forest is as shamefast as a bride,
And the forest stirs with pleasure at our far-off revelry,
And the night is filled with longing, not for all the night denied,
And the air is stirred with sighing as the winged things mate on
    high.

Come thou forth, O Venus darling! and thou Delia, retire!
For this night is not for hunting and our weapons not to slay.
Come thou forth, O Queen of Ocean, smiling at our waved fire,
Smile and make our revels daylit long beyond the death of day!

In the van of shouting lovers, many of our friends are there –
Wyatt with his charm eternal and his gift of plaintive verse,
Donne with his uneasy amours, Marlowe with his sullen air,
Keats, compact of drugs and roses, Ben, inimitably terse.

Through the woods and through the shadows, singing, the
   procession goes,
And the laughter will not slacken and the whisper will not still
Till the petals torn and scattered lose the fragrance of the rose,
Till the hand is slaked with touching and the mouth has kissed
   its fill.

Hark! they hymn the perfect goodness and the bulls in pleasure
   roar,
And the torches tossed by Cupids all the woodland creatures
   wake.
Hark! the nightingales are singing and the crying swallows soar,
And the strident-throated swans crash trumpeting above the
   lake.

Yes, they sing – but I am silent. Ah, when will my springtime be?
When shall I be as the swallow and my tongue no longer tied?
I have lost the Muse through silence. Phoebus will not look at
   me –
So Amyclae once was silent; so by her dumb spirit died.

Let them sing and dance and revel; let them kiss and slake their
   lips!
In my silence I am lonely; I have lived too late to fare
Forth among the lights and roses, where the great trees ride like
   ships,
Hated for my troubled verses, my damned twentieth century air.

KENSINGTON RIME

Miss Miffin waits by the green door
    And stays the pension guests
God help us but her mien is spare
    And eke her shrunken breasts.

She lays her skinny hand on mine
    I drop my folded Times
I cannot move no eye so glares
    Except with nameless crimes

Your eyes are blear and strange Miss Miffin
   I dread your talcumed cheek
Are you a mortal wight Miss Miffin
   Or are you faery speak

For forty years a parlous time
   I sailed in Kensington
I saw a bird a beauteous bird
   A lamp-post perched upon

Green its breast as the young plane tree
   Red its wings as a bus
Yellow its tail as the Daily Mail
   It shrieked and carolled thus

Yes like an angel's was its voice
   A bird Miss Miffin spoke
Some demon sure in the High Street
   Its rolling echoes woke

It spoke I say God be my judge
   A-lolling of its head
Mad with desire my staunch umbrella
   I raised and stabbed it dead
The beauteous creature gave one scream
   And my heart turned to lead

Now all the shoppers cried in fear
   Bitter black looks I gat
They raised the bird the beauteous bird
   And fixed it in my hat

Sore struck at heart I stumbled on
   Flaunting green yellow red
A thing foresworn outcast the brand
   Of murderer on my head

None gave me drink none gave me meat
   On every side I heard
Curse on the woman who stabbed to death
   The bird the beauteous bird

Your head is bare enough now Miss Miffin
    No shadow pales your eye
How did you lose your load Miss Miffin
    Speak woman did you die

I sailed through Paris Nice Marseilles
    Genoa Tripoli
At Wien I stuck upon a reef
    Alone in the wide wide sea

An angel lit upon my mast
    And for a moderate fee
He held my hand and pointed out
    God's monsters in the sea

Snakes in profusion walking spires
    Smooth obelisks gnarled sticks
All pulsing coloured full of blood
    I watched their kittenish tricks

I lowered down a hollow cone
    To fetch a sample up
The burden weighed a million tons
    I let the contents drop

Hopeful I lay a senseless stock
    Upon the deckboards prone
The angel murmured his regrets
    I looked and he was gone
And still the bird the beauteous bird
    Made my stufft bosom groan

Shipwreckt alone your angel gone
    You were most surely lost
I fear you perished there Miss Miffin
    And haunt this house a ghost

God in his mercy saw my plight
    And sent a paddle boat
Three days or more we seaward bore
    Then into Margate float

With dragging feet I stumbled on
   Until a lady fair
Full five feet round her generous bust
   Drew me to her warm lair

And in its darkness Rosie squeaked
   A child long dead and rotten
But though her flesh was out of mind
   Her tricks were not forgotten

She spoke me words of comfort sooth
   Out of a megaphone
And backwards would she creep and croon
   In childish tone

The room was filled with shiny heads
   Each with an aureole
They cried Rosie the great child spirit
   Hath thee in her control

I felt her cold hands at my hair
   A tearing sound I heard
And suddenly on the floor fell
   The bird the beauteous bird

I leaped up straight as light as air
   Then knelt down in the dust
I closed her eyes with banknotes five
   God will provide I trust

And oft as doth the day return
   Of my forgiven crime
I stop the first young man I meet
   And tell him all in rime

I teach him Rosie's childish prayer
   So simple and so sweet
If to do good were to do good
   Then to do good were meet.

IN MEMORIAM T.E. SHAW

Maker of kings and kingdoms; general;
Scholar; explorer; poet; these are all
Bonds that you broke, preferring slavery
Of body only. Now completely free.
Like you, we dreamed of the impossible,
But you achieved it, drank it to your fill
And then turned back to beg our sordid dress,
A hero convert to life's pettiness.
We all alike despise the multitude
But you have found some baseness in the good.
So Socrates, facing his martyr's death
Might have proved dialectic wasted breath
Or with some apt dilemma of a lyre
Shown Phaedo souls were transient as fire.
Was this to warn us that for all we strive
There's nothing worth the pain of being alive?
Or this bad world today is too distressed
To diet the adventures of the best?
We do not know, and your abandoned draft
Mocks us with our long failure at our craft.
We dare not question your delays, or ask
What you found so repugnant in your task,
For there is something in life's tactics such
That courage hamstrings hope; you had too much;
And you are deaf to question; and you lie
Far from that overbright Arabian sky
And lonely rigours of her barren strand,
Uncompromising disillusioned land,
Naked of all but courage, harsh to art,
Which offered no oasis to your heart.

Hail and farewell! We wish you, slain by chance,
The comfort of this last irrelevance.
Hail! for you raced conjecture from the start,
But as for faring well, you lacked the art;
And those who guess the springs of your distress
Can wish you nothing more than nothingness.
Not Heaven, for there's no beatitude
But your too-subtle palate would find crude;
Nor Hades, haunt of those poor piping shadows
Once heroes, who came swarming from its meadows

Lapping up the dark blood in greed to be
Again – as witness your own Odyssey –
But you would scorn such blood, and rather drink
That greasy river, hell's forgetful sink –
You who of all found the most hardly won
What most men own by birth – oblivion,
But now at last secured, as without thanks
You ply some menial office in death's ranks,
An undistinguished service that supplies
The sombre livery of your last disguise.

HEIL BALDWIN!

A Poem in celebration of the Anglo-German Naval Agreement

"The Anglo-German Agreement is the first practical move in disarmament that has been accomplished since the War."
Mr. Baldwin

  Arms and the man I sing, whose sovran power
  Has brought about at last this happy hour,
  Concord of Britain, country of the free,
  With Germany, abode of liberty.
  In pre-war days in rivalry we stood
  On either side the salt estranging flood
  Or with a child-like pleasure saw increase
  Our mighty fleets, pledges of mutual peace.
  Then, for five years, each irritated State
10 Essayed its rival to obliterate.
  Victors, we watched with a complacent eye
  The French apply the tortures of Versailles.
  In her last agonies at last repent
  And waft her present aid – at eight per cent.
  Meanwhile we all increase our armaments
  But spare poor Germany that vain expense.
  All saw to let her arm herself absurd
  As long as she would take us at our word
  But since she had ignored us, it's as plain
20 Her act must be approved to save her blame;
  For sin could be abolished in no time
  If Heaven changed the law to suit the crime.

    Until this hour the memories of the War
To perfect friendliness remained a bar.
How could our soldiers shake a hand imbrued
In many a battle with their comrades' blood?
But all can see it's more acceptable
Now that it's dipped in German blood as well.

    This ushers in the piping times of peace
When all at equal rates their arms increase;
When none dares with provoking selfishness,
Flouting its Treaties, make its army less,
Or lose the sanctions to Geneva dear
By letting guns or bombers disappear.
Needs must my Muse in her unworthy verse
The story of this miracle rehearse
And tell how rose, beneath the smiles of Fate,
Mother of Peace and Love, the Nazi State.
For all agree the seed dictates the tree –
What from *Mein Kampf* could spring but liberty?
Begin then, Muse! The Nazi State displayed:
The men who made it, and the thing they made.

    On the Great Day, ere the Third Reich began,
Before Jew's blood was banned, or Marxists' ran,
Or gallant Nazis quelled, with clubs and fists
The martial ardour of the pacifists,
Germania slept on her electoral rack
Unconscious of the doom behind her back.
A doom by Communists with such sly skill
Prepared, the world doubts they prepared it still.

    But first observe that man of iron and blood,
Von Hindenburg, whom few have understood,
After a lifetime's soldiering put by
Though charged with nothing but stupidity,
For seventy years unknown, for fifteen first
Of Germans, yet before the finish cursed.
He, when the Russian Bear-hugs first alarm,
Recalled, like Cincinnatus, from his farm,
With Hoffman's plan and Ludendorff's keen brain,
Hurls back the invader from the Eastern plain
And earns the double honours on him shed
For being a victor and a figurehead.

Let lesser generals triumph by their skill
But he by nodding and by sitting still.

   Yet to this man a genuine tribute's due,
Who, to his soldiers and his office true,
In later years steered through a stormy sea
The vessel of his vast authority,
Symbol of all that Germany once prized,
70 In duty steadfast, strong when well-advised.
This tribute History gives – and then withdraws
In the just execution of her laws.
She marks the means, but looks towards the end,
And knows, though men climb high, they may descend.
In the strange chapters of the Marshal's past
There's none so ill becomes him as the last
When for the last time to the poll he goes
By Bruening helped against his Nazi foes.
By Bruening aided, he Bruening betrays;
80 His late opponent gets the Chancellor's bays.
That oath he now reswears, a short time hence
He'll break; then die of Nazi insolence;
For even the very gods in heaven fight shy
Of virtue mingled with stupidity.
Von Hindenburg must taste the bitter pain
Of one forsworn and perjured too in vain,
Betraying Bruening and his oath of State
To save the Junker landlords from their fate:
Instead von Schleicher gasping out his life,
90 Shot like a dog, beside his slaughtered wife;
A band of gangsters apeing Junker airs
And justling generals on his very stairs;
Von Papen made the mockery of the town;
Himself a joke, his reputation gone,
A senile puppet in an emptying hall
Ducking and piping to another's call.
His second Ludendorff has learned the art
To carry off the honours of the part
And shames his marionette, with each decree
100 Extinguishing another liberty,
Till in disgust, half-groping and half-led,
He seeks at last the unreproachful dead,
All those who trusted him and trusting died,
Beaten to death or forced to suicide.

      Each action its appropriate issue breeds,
A Hitler to a Hindenburg succeeds,
Destined by heaven and some inward grace
To be the model of the Aryan race.
Like all pure Germans he is undersize,
110   Teutonically black of hair and eyes,
In person meagre and in accent shrill;
The law observing – now the law's his will.
By virtue of his unknown ancestry,
The guardian of the German race is he
And scourge of such as obstinately choose
Despite fair warning, to be born of Jews.
Yet still reveres, though by strange gods enticed,
"That greatest of all anti-Semites, Christ".

      What mocking Power, in Capital's dark days,
120   This Saviour sent, its followers to amaze?
At worst it to some logic made pretence,
Acknowledged reason, tried to utter sense,
Did homage to the moral laws it broke,
And out of Christian snippets pieced its cloak.
But this Apocalypse of our decay
All that and more besides has swept away,
For Profit's Prophet, impudently dense,
Has summoned ignorance to its defence,
Has reconditioned and bedizened it
130   With fables, manias, lies surpassing wit,
Queer morals, comic art, false history,
Bankrupt religion, dead philosophy,
Which, like its vamped-up gods, are neither new,
Nor plausible, nor – till this era – true,
But true they are now, spite of sense and reason.
Nazi decrees have made their falsehood treason,
And all admit those arguments have force
Which have it as their principal resource.
No wonder, then, an earlier capitalist
140   Should be regretful at what he has missed,
For he had always thought that insolence
Must be disguised with a parade of sense,
That one should reason with the multitude
And show them they are robbed for their own good,
Until our Saviour Hitler's simpler brain
Perceived this trouble was completely vain,

  That nations can be impudently tricked,
Those few that have the wit to see it kicked,
Robbed openly of clothes, sense, food, and leisure,
150 Driven to work and then dragooned to pleasure.

   Now millions more, work longer hours – for less
Than what they drew before in idleness –
For has not every German got the right
To such necessities as dynamite?
Why need he make what might exchange for bread
When he proposes a free gift of – lead?
Why forge a bicycle when he can cast
The guns by which he'll, blasting, others blast?
A shame indeed if in a time of need
160 He should to creature comforts give his heed!
No, let him work, and die if he protest,
Gaoled without trial, or from sheer spite oppressed,
Forbid to speak, to think, to read, to hear,
Taught good by cruelty, courage by fear,
Dizzy from discipline and crazed with hate –
All for that abstract unknown thing, a State,
Which none has seen, and few so impudent
As to suppose themselves by it are meant.
For plainly the object of their sacrifice
170 Is their own leaders' luxury and vice.

   This is the Nazi Saviour's Holy Writ,
Preposterous enough to silence wit.
For Adolf Hitler, its evangelist,
Von Hindenburg his counsellor dismissed.
Since the effect casts on the cause its blame
Von Hindenburg thus earned undying shame.
Yet History asks – still curious of the soul –
Does Hitler his own rubbish swallow whole?
More than a fool if he can thus believe;
180 Worse than a fiend if he would thus deceive.

   Nor must his henchmen be forgotten here:
Goering, and Goebbels his uneasy peer.
Goering, who it would be unjust to say
Was nothing but a bully in decay,
A loudmouthed barrel fired with drugs and drink,
Able to bellow, strut, all things but think,

Who had but one idea his life long –
That he was of importance – and that wrong;
An actor whose conceited bluster tries
In uniforms his grossness to disguise,
Who once possessed the courage of the brute,
Violent in rage, in malice resolute,
But now, by luxury and praise unmanned
Prefers to risk his life at second-hand
And with a choice Pretorian guard of toughs
Directs the tactics of brave S.A. roughs,
So careful of the peace that when they've done
A murder or a rape, they cut and run,
And never fight unless they're ten to one;
Too gentle to assault the pacifists
Until they safely manacled their wrists;
Too kind to kill their prisoners till they've tried
By torture to procure their suicide.

    Who'll dare assert, despite his ill repute,
That Goering's nothing but this brainless brute?
Who would not scorn such a preposterous shell?
Who would not fear it if it had brains as well?

    His colleague is a different pair of shoes,
Goebbels, whom none of brainlessness accuse.
Like those familiar spirits prompt at hand
To drain a sea or spin a rope from sand,
Able to do all things his masters will,
On one condition – that they are for ill.
Why are such powerful devils always slaves,
Servants of simple fools as well as knaves?
Is it their cowardice that keeps them down,
For all their cunning, trembling at a frown?
Or is it that Earth's forces own control
Only to creatures that can lose a soul?

    So far we've seen the Nazi's outward grin
But now we look upon the thing within;
Its meagre malice, its destructive art,
The lust for power of its envious heart,
Repleted monster, coiled around its prize,
Whom Goebbels taught, encouraged, fed with lies.
He guided Hitler from his earliest hour;

>
> He pointed out the tedious path to power;
> He planned the victory, a rape on Fate,
> And now has his reward: contempt and hate.
> Such men none loves, yet none dares do without,
> Ignored in triumph, scapegoats in a rout.
> He by his arts all Germany deceived,
> Now by all lied to, and by few believed:
> So fit to teach poor devils to rebel
> He could change for the worse the rule of Hell.
>
>   With these were others, farther from the throne,
> Who all the party's varying lot had known,
> Whose friends and followers oft heard Hitler boast
> Of what he'd do when he should rule the roast.
> Hitler, for long, too kind of heart to blame,
> With Christian meekness bore their evil fame:
> Their luxury, their well-known vice, their pride –
> The shirt such peccadilloes sanctified –
> But all agreed it was the outside edge
> When some reminded him of his old pledge.
> Then it was time to stop the moral rot;
> Immediately two hundred odd were shot.
> Those still survive who only morals lacked,
> But it was fatal to be short of tact.
>
>   While Hindenburg still lived, and Adolf loved
> The Chief of Staff he later had removed,
> While Hitler, Chancellor, seemed a simple dupe,
> A prisoner of the tiny Junker group,
> While Nazis, with a shrinking vote, saw loom
> In the elections six days hence their doom,
> Sudden and dreadful on the brow of night
> The darkened Reichstag glowed with fiery light.
> A pile of massive stone, its granite shell
> Was filled with flame, the Council Hall a hell.
> Two men had seen the conflagration start
> And through the flames a frenzied figure dart.
> They urged a policeman to desert his place
> Who unenthusiastically gave chase.
> The flying figure crashed through panes of glass.
> Their bullets missed. He has escaped alas!
> But by now Goering, summoned to the spot,
> A revelation straight from God has got.

Before he goes inside the truth he sees:
"The Communists are the incendiaries.
270   This beacon will their evil purpose light.
No loyal German will be safe tonight."
This Goering said; this Goering still believes
For who would dare suppose that God deceives?
Or that, like Nazi justice, Providence
Cannot at will with evidence dispense?
The land remained wrapped in accustomed peace.
The moment failed its horrors to release.
Goering himself, where Heavenly Power falls short
Will see God's warning is not brought to naught!
280   Since blood He promised why then, blood will run,
And all things, as foretold by Him, be done.

Meanwhile to Helldorff, many miles apart,
God deigns like inspiration to impart.
At once he sets storm-troopers to their task.
With zeal they work beneath night's sable mask.
Ere Germany awakes to a new day
Five thousand rebels have been put away –
For, by a strange presentiment of Fate,
Helldorff had guessed this danger to the State
290   A month before, and made a detailed list
Of every future-guilty Communist
And (showing how unbiased were his views)
Included also pacifists and Jews.
Later, denying his angelic aid,
Helldorff recounted how the list was made –
How in a raid upon the Red H.Q.
The whole plan of rebellion came to view –
But since he never showed these documents
All reckon this mere pious reticence;
300   For had he known the Reichstag might be fired,
Plainly an extra guard would be required
But since they had been warned of nothing odd,
His prescience could only come from God.

    Apart from this, the night passed quiet away.
Only a groan or two disturbed the day
Where, blending private joys with public weal
Affronted Nazis made their victims squeal –
Perhaps old friends whom they owed money to,

  Or well-known Marxists, or an unknown Jew:
310 Or else the calm was troubled by the tramp
  Of limping rebels marching to a camp –
  Kind forethought! for in some deserted part
  Their screams will not disturb a tender heart.

  Now Germany discovers the dire fate
  From which the Nazis have preserved the State.
  Alas! at first she doubts. For such is sin
  A Saviour's hardest task has always been
  Not to convince he plays a Saviour's part
  But that men needed saving at the start.
320 Later, their Saviour every German sees.
  None but a Saviour'd take such liberties –
  The liberties of speech, of hearing, thought,
  Of writing anything, believing aught,
  Till in due course the Reichstag with full state
  Will freedom's self gravely obliterate
  And when the final right of man's suppressed
  With Christian meekness vote itself *non est*.
  In vain now let a cunning Marxist plot
  Against the Reichstag, for the Reichstag's not.
330 Instead see perfect peace reign willy-nilly
  Where all who disagree are beaten silly.
  How free from party strife smiles hill and dale
  When all the other parties are in gaol!
  Where can such sweet unanimity be found
  Except where every critic's underground?
  Who would not such restraining vigour choose
  When in return he can torment the Jews
  Or demonstrating Nazi valour, beat
  Some solitary stranger in the street?
340 Who cannot see the value of the Group
  When, bent on rape or flogging, out they troop
  And vindicate the manhood of their race
  By punching made-up women in the face.

  But we anticipate. Goering still stares
  At the black ruin and its fitful flares.
  Hitler and Goebbels (who, chance fortunate!
  This evening are together, dining late)
  Are hurrying to the scene, and far away
  Helldorff prepares his Aryan holiday;

350   When, sudden, Goering hears a joyful cry:
"The police have captured the incendiary".
They bring the captive. Lubbe; shock-haired; wild;
Half-blind, half-naked, dribbling like a child.
"I fired the Reichstag", was all he could say –
"I, and I only", till his dying day.
The man was bare of tell-tale documents –
Except a passport, useful evidence!
Puzzling; but still one fact could not be missed.
This van der Lubbe was a Communist.
360   This revelation Goering had received
Direct from God, and God must be believed.

   The hall and corridors they search with care.
Except for van der Lubbe, not a hair!
Until a Deputy (Albrecht by name)
At ten o'clock comes rushing from the flame,
Hatless and coatless, full of panic fear.
The police arrested him. All looked severe.
Interrogated, porters testified
Albrecht had been at least two hours inside.
370   The fire however started after eight!
Albrecht will surely meet a tragic fate!
But "Hold!" he cries. "I am a Nazi. It
Is certain this by Communists was lit.
Therefore I must be guiltless." The police saw
This proposition was without a flaw,
For police and politicians have known long
That those who hold the power can do no wrong.
The porter's reprimanded for his lies,
Albrecht's released with full apologies,
380   And with the dangerous captive closely bound
The glad procession leaves the fatal ground.

   Now seven months go by. All think it time
The criminals should suffer for their crime.
The more since in the intervening season
It retrospectively becomes high treason.
As plotters are essential to a plot,
The Government the necessary's got –
The three Bulgarians, the ex-Deputy,
And the young Dutchman, lost in phantasy –
390   So queer a bunch, so contrary to sense

All recognise the need of evidence,
And seven months was barely enough time
To find some testimony of the crime,
But still the prosecution's zeal was such
The fault was, not too little, but too much;
A hundred witnesses saw the accused's faces
At the same time – but each in different places,
Or hatching treason all in the same spot,
But in each case it was a different plot.
400 That all was said about the accused was true
They knew for sure, but this was all they knew,
Not sure of when they saw these men, or where,
Or how they looked, but sure of who they were.
For all its farce, the trial's remembered yet,
For with the jests were things we'll not forget.
We'll not forget, in freedom's darkest hour
How Dimitroff's courage triumphed over power,
And in the teeth of Nazi violence
Confounded them with their own evidence.
410 In vain they wriggle, bluster, threaten, gloze,
Each lie of theirs another will expose.
For fifty-seven days the tedious farce
Through every stage of ridicule must pass
Till as the comedy reels to its close,
All Europe the real guilty party knows.

From the first day even a Nazi eye
Could find no flaw in Dimitroff's alibi –
Who while the Reichstag fell in fiery rain
Was sitting in the Munich-Berlin train;
420 But, scorning prudence or forensic art,
Dimitroff, man of no ordinary heart,
Defied his captors; with a wink or joke
Silenced false witness; and made Goering choke.
Expelled five times from court, each time returned
With some fresh tactic from the lawyers learned
With which to countermine the sapping law
And blast with ridicule its hollow awe.
His courage to his co-accused he lends;
Their lives from their defenders he defends,
430 And at the end, acquitted of the crime,
Demands a compensation for lost time.
Helpless and dumb the Nazi cabal stands;

Its engine has exploded in its hands.
Now, thanks to Dimitroff's gallant impudence
The prosecution becomes a defence,
And growing preposterous with fury, tries
To justify its lying with more lies.
But tries in vain, for Taneff never knew
German, and Popoff but a word or two,
440 While both must speak to their conspirator,
The German Torgler, by interpreter,
And many think, where plotters cannot speak
To one another, that their plot is weak.

    But though the trial a comedy becomes,
Behind it grim reality still looms: –
Seven months of prison, manacled, abused,
With all the famous Nazi kindness used;
Small wonder Torgler meeker tactics tried,
And Taneff, dumb, attempted suicide;
450 But neither blows nor fetters could control
Dimitroff's revolutionary soul,
Who, warned by Goering of a certain death,
Retorts his threats, and still expounds his faith,
Well able – what no tyrant e'er forgives –
To argue for the faith by which he lives.

    But what of van der Lubbe, who confessed –
As police detectives solemnly attest –
With flowers of speech, with zeal that warms the heart,
In fluent German full of vocal art?
460 All through the trial he bows his shaggy head,
As limp and senseless as a man half-dead,
Or staggering to his feet, in broken Dutch
Mouths gibberish – this man who talked so much.
Yet none the less, his statement being read
The court gets "Yes" or "No" on every head
And though half of his answers make no sense,
The other half confirm the evidence.
At intervals, like a piece learned by rote,
He lifts his head and mutters in his throat:
470 "I fired the Reichstag". – "That is all I know".
"How, why, or when I know not; but it's so".

      His history might touch a tender heart.
Fate had small mercy on him from the start.
Injured, half-blinded, strangely drawn to roam
On his small pittance, far from friend and home;
Some local workers' party joins, then leaves.
None knows, least he himself, what he believes.
Yet, driven to action by his dumb distress,
Has arson often tried, without success.
480 Few would suppose this dreamer gone to seed,
With "voices in his body", fit to plead,
But Nazi experts find a perfect brain,
Pronounce the slavering tramp completely sane,
And swear his isolation and distress
Are just a passing fit of sulkiness.

      How did he enter the well-guarded hall,
Unless he could traverse a solid wall?
One answer and one only had been found;
That he was smuggled in there underground.
490 A tunnel joins (happy convenience!)
The Reichstag with the Speaker's residence.
But Goering was the Speaker and this way
Was guarded by storm-troopers on the Day.
If down this tunnel van der Lubbe went
The consequence is fairly evident.

      The experts swore, no man, unhelped, could raise
In so few moments such a blistering blaze –
Unless indeed the fire had been prepared –
But then who did so, passed the Nazi guard.
500 Who could have led this half-blind dreaming fool
Down the dark tunnel, an unconscious tool,
And left him there, confronted by the deed,
Which seemed from his own action to proceed,
Alone, confused, with voices in his head,
But claiming the glory of the fire he'd raised
With the warped egoism of the crazed?
Those only who'd both means and motive got!
If this were true, it was a Nazi plot.
But Dollfuss slaughtered soon in Austria
510 Should prove their hatred for all *coups d'état*,
And who, regarding Goebbel's honest face,
Hitler's kind smile, or Goering's gentle grace,

111

Could dream such crafty-childish plotting true?
Only a Marxist, Pacifist, or Jew!

    Well, silent still, unconscious of his fate,
Or dumb from idiot courage, see him wait.
The trial is ending. Europe's expectation
Awaits justice's final vindication.
The court returns. We bow. They bow. All sit.
Torgler and the Bulgarians we acquit!
Europe rejoices. Accents loud and shrill.
In German Leipzig there are judges still!
But wait. One verdict has not yet been read:
The van der Lubbe boy must lose his head.
This lubber idiot, for his harmless jest –
A demonstration of disgust at best –
Must suffer that extremest penalty
Created by a subsequent decree.
Hail Justice! who this youth still wrapped in cloud
Leads shambling, manacled, his shock-head bowed
Like some enormous yet pathetic ape,
Out to the block at dawn. Now on his nape,
The executioner (his charms displayed
In tail coat and white gloves) brings down the blade.
The head rolls, stops, and up to Heaven stares;
The face its chubby-idiot look still wears:
And Lubbe has redeemed at this high rate
The Act on which was reared the Nazi State:
Yes, on an idiot's corpse this thing was built.
Its secret to secure, his blood was spilt.
If any God there were, with genial eye
Watching the sparrows and exploited die,
This deed should bring his thunders rattling down.
But none observed the face of Heaven frown.

    Torgler meanwhile, for being innocent,
In prison suffers two years' punishment,
For in the Nazi state those who to crime
Add an acquittal, have the harder time.
Since wrongful gaoling scorn for justice breeds
The verdict the indictment now precedes,
And later Torglers, innocent of fame
Vanish, and no one even hears their name,
Their friends and families left for many a year

Too wise to hope, too ignorant to despair.
When to be prosecuted is a crime
Is not a trial and verdict waste of time?
The public headman's not used every day.
"Shot while escaping" is a cheaper way.
When this device too often has been tried
560 Repeated torture ends in suicide.
In vain to lands more civilised they fly,
By Nazis dragged across the boundary!

   No apt Mons angels wait, with starry eyes
To save you, captives, from your agonies,
Though many a tender vegetarian soul
May drop a tear for you – still the heads roll.
The League protests, but pacifists are trained
To grasp a proffered hand, however stained.
The arts are helpless, like the sciences,
570 Expelled, they rush to us as refugees.
Ex-soldiers, who at least would sometimes fly
In war's red hell the rags of chivalry
Are now but tolerated at the best
By these new knights. The Stalhelm is suppressed.
And God himself, so far from helping you,
Is pushed from heaven by the Nazi crew,
Thus by no scraps of law or faith concealed
The gangster Nazidom now stands revealed.
Then do you turn to us, land of the free,
580 Proud of our heritage of liberty,
Long pledged to free the spinning world from slaves,
(And tolerate no rival on the waves)?
Alas, poor souls! The point you've sadly missed.
Baldwin is nothing if not Nationalist.
Like Hitler, he too had his Reichstag day
But in a far more gentlemanly way.
Our van der Lubbe – Ramsay – is not dead.
He lives; although it's true he lost his head.
To do things in a decent way's our pride.
590 He was not kicked to death but kicked aside.
All must admit that our gold standard scare
Was as effective as a Reichstag flare
And Socialists are much more impotent
When prisoned in that maze, a Parliament.
Why wield the butcher's axe, Brutality,

When we've the surgeon's knife, Economy?
Therefore our Liberal – Labour – Nationalists
Embrace the coarser Nazi-Socialists.
Their manners are not nice; their ways are crude,
600 But to ignore them would be rather rude.
And though the means they chose we needs must blame
The end we welcome, for our end's the same;
And now in amity let us both steer
To greater things each national career –
To larger navies, in proportion due,
Armies and air forces forever new,
Forever growing, which forever bring
A larger dividend with each new spring.
What matter for whom Nazis sharp their knives?
610 Can England die while Capital still lives?
What matter though the Fascists civilise
Dark Ethiopia? Don't we sympathise?
But let's step in before they take the whole
And share the market we cannot control,
The way in far Manchuria we found
To hunt the hare yet run before the hound,
And if we get insulted here and there,
We are not proud, we are not what we were,
But like St. Paul, being all things to all men,
620 Trade with the lands whose methods we condemn.

    Where God, the League, justice, abuse, and prayer
And even kindness fails, must you despair.
You captives, hidden from the light of day?
You workers, free to toil, yet crushed as they?
No! Unimpassioned as the changing sky
Resolves the dialectic, History,
And Nazidom, afraid for all its art
Feels the sharp contradictions at its heart,
While Revolution, dumb, its leaders gone,
630 Despite all this more violently lives on.
Still, underground, forbidden papers pass
And voice the wrongs of the exploited class;
Still Lenin's wisdom and the thought of Marx
Burn steadily, and spread, and send up sparks,
And this time, sudden as the Reichstag fright,
No building, but a people see alight!

>In those bright flames, presage of brighter day,
>The rubbish of these years will melt away
>And, like a man from nightmare glad to wake,
>This land will see the dawn, the red dawn, break,
>And over ruined Nazidom unfurled
>The second banner of the classless world.

from *Poems* (1939)
1934-1936

EPITAPH

Unhappy men, who roam, on hope deferred
   Relying, thinking not of painful death!
Here was Seleucos, great in mind and word,
   Who his young prime enjoyed for but a breath.
In world-edge Spain, so far from Lesbian lands
   He lies, a stranger on uncharted strands.

From the Latin

THE HAIR

This hair, I took it first for tidiness
And then for love (for it is valueless)
And knotting it around my button said:
When you and I are dead
This hair may still be living. They'll not find
What Donne prospected, round the bare bone twined
This filament; it may be anywhere.
A mouse may steal it to line his cold lair;
Some bald apothecary full of hope
May stretch the strand across his microscope;
Or a new turn of fashion's wheel, of which
We've seen so many, may make a girl stitch
The golden thread in her embroidery;
Or simply this bright hair will simply be.

You never felt the loss. It quietly fell
Yet had I plucked it, would have made you yell,
And I too being torn from you, you'd weep,
But what I fear is, I'll slide from your keep
As other men have done, I know it well
And none will value what so easily fell
But some sly mouse or a short-sighted maid
Who hums and shades with hair her curious braid.

This was a part of you until it went
Which now doctors but rate as excrement;
And in my vision, blessed because mine,
This trifle shone too, thin but present line

For nothing that was you was missed. That gone
This hair is all my hope can fatten on;
And even if I had as much of hair
As – when we embraced to the cool sheets bare –
Slipped from your brow to mine, it's not all you.
It is not nearly you. I'd take in lieu
Of you perhaps your letter, promise, heart
(You owe a heart). But I'll reject a part
For not a million parts can make the you
That my desires phantastically pursue.

Ah, when I'm bald, and love becomes disgust
(Your love will last up to that date I trust
But cannot know) you cannot imp on me
The years or hairs you now give easily.
No, for my girl at that not-distant date
You will unwillingly render to Fate
Each gift he asks back: hair, smooth skin, bright eyes,
The brave spring of your bosom, your curved thighs.
It's Beauty that falls from you; that I wind
Around my button, and I call to mind
Libations which the prudent pagans shed
Out of their plenty to the gods of dread,
For so this strand. But Time will strip you bare.
Me too. We'll shiver in the spiky air.
Ev'n flesh will go at last. Time will expose
This wig of flesh we wear from pate to toes
And pick our very bones bare. This first hair
Must for its draughty end our love prepare.
So clip and clip me! I can keep you warm
As long as any man can stave off harm;
At least I promise beauty will not fall
As this hair fell, unfought, unnoticed; all
Time plucks from you will send an exquisite
Pain through us both; I'll hold and hold you tight
And make him tug our flesh off. They will find
No hairy bracelet round your wristbone tied
For not until all moveables have gone
Shall I give up to Death your skeleton;
Not even then, for round your ribs will be
The bare arms of my own anatomy.

HYMN TO PHILOSOPHY

I saw your figure in a Grecian mode:
A stripling with the quiet wings of death,
Touching with your long fingers a marble lyre.

I was impressed by your immortal age,
I was seduced by your adventurous strength,
I was relieved by your polite reserve.

A winged Idea down the rainbow sliding,
With steady steps treading the smoky air,
All ranks you visit, courteous swamp-foul.

The world's great engines pound asthmatically
Fed through Time's hopper by recurrences
Man walks to man across a trembling swamp.

The scientific sportsman lifts his gun;
The second barrel blasts your blue pin-feathers
And you fall spluttering, a specific bird.

I see your stuffed breast and boot-button eyes
Preserved in cases for posterity
And lean on my umbrella thoughtfully.

I have caressed your sort, I must confess,
But give me beauty beauty that must end
And rots upon the taxidermist's hands.

TIERRA DEL FUEGO

When our full-bosomed ship drave through the Straits,
Our eyeballs frozen with continual watch,
A Diego said: "In those chill-swirling waters
What monsters move, rolling beneath our keel!"

And at his words the hoarse bird-bearing night
Blazed with sharp fires, in rank seraphic ranged,
An orderly regression of bright eyes
That watched us. Voiceless company of comets...

"An angel stands by each, tending with art
His steady flame, his curled brows bent in thought,
Ingeminating some creative hymn,"
So said our captain, in his gallery kneeling.

"With menial breath each puffs his fervour up,
And these will watch us till we fetch the point
And, wearing ship, stand for the north again.
Look that you keep your hearts and speeches clean."

"No," muttered our arquebusier in his beard,
"A devil, shapen like a rocky hill,
Gorged with the larded flesh of heretics,
Spirts out these touch-flares from his creviced hide."

Dawn came. Landing, priest-guarded, for fresh water
We found some naked manlings, foul as monkeys,
Who shivered, squatting in their holes of filth,
And cast opprobrious rubbish; till we charged.

Mere brutes they knelt, revering Christian giants.
A few we spitted on our swords; the rest
Our priests whipped till they owned the Christ; one girl
Ape-faced, but breasted well, our captain took.

WAS IT?

Was it mere manners
To practise that deft flexion of white wrists
That gave the ruffles their hypnotic grace?

Was it lasciviousness to send
The dishes in to those seductive tunes
Lest the words stumbled on the slippery floor?

Was it no more than repartee
To wind the question in neat folds
Then lay it bare with one uncoiling gesture?

If so, I was a hollow man
A decently-articulated doll,
I was no poet, plump with fire and blood

And you will hear a crash of falling glass
And find me (sawdust welling from the wound)
Stabbed through the bosom by the dirty truth.

Outside the nightingales (bemoaning me)
Tear their brown breasts; and the June roses moult.
Open the window and throw down a coin.

DONNE'S REVERIE

Oh let your faces beaming in the smoke
Haunt me in death, when lungs and spirit choke
And, putting by with a fantastic hand
The friends who'd wind me in cerecloths, I stand
And contemplate around the sallow wrist
(Fall, memories fall!) the bright thin hairy twist,
Remembering how our heads the violets pressed
– A bosomy bank, love's softly-fragrant nest –
All a day through; palm grew then into palm
Cemented by a soft soul-sucking balm,
And the sun's ruddy face through curtains thrust
Looked enviously on our skeletal lust.

No matter, I have seen at the world's end
The weary planets from their cars descend
But I have never seen woman with soul.
Her flesh I count worth only as a goal
That quenches my desire; yet she's a queen
And in the dark her tressy crown is seen
Potable gold! To bed. The hunt is on
And we'll not bait until the deed is done,
For each such makes our span of living less;
Out to the brink our sweaty chargers press;
We meditate on what commodious way
Should love's bare godhead take a holiday.

I have wasted, lean-shanked, all hair and bone
That have the globed breasts of young women known.
They're dead: now praise the sweet nut-brown beldame
Weaving a sheet of beauty round her shame
And when she's dead, I squeeze the grapy earth
To praise her, sacred in it gave her birth
But then regretted having lost its name
Recalled her, infamously gaining fame.

But I too wither; in the springs of hell
I smell the breath that I conceit too well.
Too well! Thus loneliness. Thus hell. Retreat.
The soul. Alone. No more. The last conceit.
Go deeper still! Let any woman rot,
The devil's snares, that are all that is not,
Ripe with the fragrance of immortal sheets,
In love's war tired with delightful defeats;
But swear they cheat you, courtier out-at-heels
Who thinks, smirks, hates, rhymes, rattles: yes and feels!

Dig to the roots! You have rehearsed your death
And scraped from poor vain glass your crusted breath.
A million texts, like white signposts at night,
Point point the way; on each rests your cracked sight.
But wait. Wait till these crowds of words have gone.
See, more and more. Death clatters. You have done.

THE STONES OF RUSKIN

A lion with grey hair and fragile hands
Ruskin, that lover of right-living art,
Towards the long end of a saintly life,
Forsaking the decorous slim-waisted Misses
Of a Greek-Oxfordised mythology
Stepped absent-mindedly into a boat
Which bore him to that Land of Women, sung
In Trobriand Island records of the gods.
These fell on him, libidinous and strong,
Abused him, roused him, stroked him, drove him mad.
A little while his roars of pain were heard

Echoing from Rydal and the fell-grey steeps.
Then he was dead, champing the spring-fed grass,
His spirit at the bottom of the lake
Cold and disastrous of virginity.

We need not laugh, although all saw how pat
And apt it was this harpy Nemesis
Should catch the organ-voiced old maid of art.
Such foul enchantments wait for all us bards.
Some few in garrets starved or blue gulfs drowned
Are lucky ones, taken in youthful bloom.
Some in dress suits, protective mimicry,
Succeed in imitating business men
And the hawk Furies baffled pass them over.
The wisest stop their gambols and become
As ease stops up the operative glands
Sleek, ox-eyed, ruminative gelded beasts
Or at the worst drift off the stage of life
The slobber-lipped and palsied clowns of age.
All others come to curse the thing they blessed
And daub their chains with filth or scream at night,
Whipped by all the fat devils out of hell
Until their brother-madmen stop their mouths.

CLASSIC ENCOUNTER

Arrived upon the downs of asphodel
I walked towards the military quarter
To find the sunburnt ghosts of allied soldiers
Killed on the Chersonese.

I met a band of palefaced weary men
Got up in odd equipment. "Hi," I said
"Are you Gallipoli?"

And one, the leader, with a voice of gold,
Answered: "No. Ours, Sir, was an older bungle.
We are Athenian hoplites who sat down
Before young Syracuse.

"Need I recount our too-much-memoired end?
The hesitancy of our General Staff,
The battle in the Harbour, where Hope fled
But we could not?

"Not our disgrace in that," the leader added,
"But we are those proficient in the arts
Freed in return for the repeated verses
Of our Euripides.

"Those honeyed words did not soothe Cerberus"
(The leader grinned), "For sulky Charon hire
Deficient, and by Rhadamanthos ruled
No mitigation.

"And yet with men, born victims of their ears
The chorus of the weeping Troades
Prevailed to gain the freedom of our limbs
And waft us back to Athens.

"Through every corridor of this old barracks
We wander without friends; not fallen or
Survivors in a military sense:
Hence our disgrace."

He turned; and as the rank mists took them in
They chanted of the God to Whom men pray,
Whether He be Compulsion, or All-Fathering,
Or Fate and blind.

THE PROGRESS OF POETRY

I saw a Gardener with a watering can
Sprinkling dejectedly the heads of men
Buried up to their necks in the wet clay.

I saw a Bishop born in sober black
With a bewildered look on his small face
Being rocked in a cradle by a grey-haired woman.

I saw a man, with an air of painful duty
Binding his privates up with bunches of ribbon.
The woman who helped him was decently veiled in white.

I said to the Gardener: "When I was a younger poet
At least my reference to death had some sonority.
I sang the danger and the deeps of love.

"Is the world poxy with a fresh disease?
Or is this a maggot I feel here, gnawing my breast
And wrinkling my five senses like a walnut's kernel?"

The Gardener answered: "I am more vexed by the lichen
Upon my walls. I scraped it off with a spade.
As I did so I heard a very human scream.

"In evening's sacred cool, among my bushes
A Figure was wont to walk. I deemed it angel.
But look at the footprint. There's hair between the toes!"

ESSAY ON FREEWILL

Our deeds are broken horns of glass
Cast on the cold Atlantic shores
Where the indifferent breakers pass
Write your revenge on the white doors
The white huts of a leisured class.

And Newton in his spider's den
Forsaking the delights of love
Is broken broken City men
Haunt the deserted temple grove
And strike the hours upon Big Ben.

What's done is done is done is done
My father's father fat with sin
Will feel no flesh will see no sun

Our vain regrets are dinosaurs
Infesting coalseams of the hours
Our hopes as fast as time can spin
Pressed up in calf-bound books like flowers

Remember me when I am dead
The last thing that Napoleon said

THE COAL

Lay it not out extravagantly
This red-hot coal we bear between our thighs.
Time's chastening airs make eunuch of our hopes:
Poor spendthrift perish not in bankruptcy.

    Twice one is two is two is two
    This farthing wisdom I have learned.
    Turn the page over; note the sum,
    And carry one, and carry one.

    Blow into flame O Holy Ghost
    The secret womb by thought made dull
    To the toad's guarded brow entrust
    The jewelled organ, fruitfulness.

I choose to spend it on my comrades; choose
To lavish it on ignorant citizens.
I choose to warm with this hard-wrested gem
The conversations of the draughty streets.

    Goddess of passionate chastity
    No man can make a living thus.
    The land will see our dwindlers starve
    And lose its pregnant dividend.

    The loins that tree-like strip them bare
    Will perish of their poverty,
    The plough hand-lacking rest and rust
    And long-productive wells run dry.

Then damn all profit perish all increase
It is not love that reckons by the book.
Such warmth we own let life's cold pilgrims sup
Come! on the shivering margent of the tides

Let us haul hearty, knee to knee,
And pull the whey-faced shipwracked in,
To piece among their nakedness our clothes
And in our bosoms warm their bitterness.

TWENTY SONNETS OF WM. SMITH

I

Come live with me and be my love.
Let us love's bourgeois pleasures prove
Where grasses' homely knitting spreads
Antimacassars for the hill's heads
Or landlady, shrill-rattled snake,
Glides through the aspidistran brake.
Let us be honest, flesh is flesh,
Yet there's a difference in the dish
If spiced with natural pleasantries
Or raw upon the slab life-size.
Where shall we fry our dish of love
And its more subtle pleasures prove?
   You know love is as we are able;
   The dish is done when brought to table.

II

Before us all who worked this leaping oar
Contrived to drench the handle with perfume
But we in Love's hot galley load the grain
With natural sweat that bites the kissing palm.
Let words drip honey and drunk lovers pledge
Their raptures in the rose's cleanly breast,
Our own employ will have a rougher edge
In its own liquors by our lips confessed,

Shameless of whence it sucked its raw delights,
As sailors in their rough and tarry mode
Announce what grand extraordinary sights
Are to their nest of stinking cabins owed
   Concealing not the thing by which they move.
   Old body, faithful vessel of our love.

III

If I obscure the flesh's endless shout
With patterns of a stale complexity
Admit me no excuse and no regret,
Traitor to you and traitor to our love.
If I betray our passion's simple gust
With flavourings of vaporous romance
May I be damned to burn in hell with lust
And find how these vague bubbles flee my lips;
But if I have exacerbated sense
To ape the soul's deep suction of delight,
If I have staggered with polyvalence
The fantasies that scorch our giddy eyes
   And shocked the slippery habitudes of night
   Count it as merit and a poet's right.

IV

S to which mind ascribes the P of beauty!
Class of all classes patient to desire!
Let me pay learning and its conjuring tricks
The verbal homage of delirium,
And when we write that all-or-nothing h
In which we nothing do; or utterly
Expend our energy to glut our breasts
Let me profane my lips with algebra.
The ten co-ordinates of space achieved
The moment's miracle I sum as you
And tired of roses, eyes, superfluous stars
I praise you with the filthy rags of time.
   With universes, galaxies, those tracts
   Of death that wait to drink our limbs and acts.

V

We are not what songs feign, my love my rose,
But beings full of blood and filthiness
And we must cram as desperately as beasts
The increment of our experience.
Each day is a concession to despair,
Each look, sigh, hope, delusion's armoury
And while Pygmalion smooths his frigid stone,
Insultingly betraying love's hot smell,
Let us squeeze with the furious haste of greed
The utmost brightness from our clipping limbs
Until the body's pulp distills its tears,
Salt, sweet, the tribute of our peach-fed love,
   Pressed from this fatty garment we have on,
   Joys foreign to the decent skeleton.

VI

Lift the church and find the altar;
Lift the altar; find the stone:
Lift the stone and find the toad;
Lift the toad and find the rock.

I heaved the rock up, heaved like hell,
I pulled the rock up by the roots;
I pulled a church up by the hair:
Church and altar; stone and toad.

We found the occupation childish,
And while the organ, solemn, godlike,
Pealed out of the stained-glass windows
We fornicated to its tune.
Jones, more mystic, with a groan
Bashed his brains out on the stone.

VII

Let the lovely birds and beasts
Explicate our common love;
How we lovers link our hopes
Faithfullest of living things.

Let the spider and his mate
That digestive passion can
Sing the praise of constancy
Each to each; it were a wonder.

Neither can the other part,
Each embracing, each embraced –
Never two so dear and common.
Now no fly can come between.

No butterfly with violent wings
Flattering the sun and airs of spring
Win one's bright regard from other;
Never were such true-loves seen.

> Here they lie; who knew love; could apply it;
> If they grew bored, they could each other diet.
> He made one dinner; she a little tried
> To live without more; liked it not; and died.

VIII

Though rulers fall and nations perish
Love's principality stands firm,
Its feet four-square upon the floor;
The floor upon the living rock.

Sweet fields of hay by yokels pressed
Or water buoying the cow whale
The earth indifferently sustains
On her basaltic carapace.

Religion fades; art is a dream,
Philosophy is bored to death;
But while the globe is sound at heart
Its beams will bear a lover's weight.

And gravity is with us yet
Lest we forget, lest we forget.

IX

The nightingale! it only needed that –
For this ex-reptile of an old-wives' tale
With her lost only asset maidenhead
To caterwaul into the sweaty night.
I have worshipped this animal I must admit,
Perched on many a thoughtful page, revealing
Lonely headlands, scraped by whispering clouds
And those great bumpers, filled with heady wine!
But now when I walk out to cool my head
Having tried to suck some sweetness from her breasts
And turn the greasy book of love anew,
My plucked nerves trembling with a stale delight
   I hear this proclamation, rarely heard:
   It's chance. You cannot know, gossiping bird!

X

In your bran lists of love no firstling tilter
I lease your bed from many able wights
Who to the tourney have rehearsed my part
Better than I perhaps; I am not vain
Nor would I now reproach your openness
With any civil breach of guarantee.
The best is ripe; yours is no colic love
Nor rail I at those ghosts our converse warms,
And yet I rail, tenacious of my dream
In which I saw our only images
Like swan and shadow solitary drawn
Across the virgin belly of a lake,
   Restless in rest because my poet's heart
   Secretes a chasteness proper to my art.

XI

What is your essence, how can you have purged
Your being of the ghosts that I evoked?
A million flowers uselessly tinged my brain
If your warm skin recalls no other scent.
Helen's advertisement was so much waste,
Your proper features can blot out her looks.

And ladies linking deftly chains of days
With which to lap the shins of hero-knights
Superfluous labour with their long white hands
Since your economy ensnared my soul.
Yes, you are you; you flaunt the naked fact
And mock my dream-soaked youth with all its waste.
  It is your trick or right and warns me well,
  Dream as I may, you will be what you are.

XII

Tritons lift shells, the grapy bubbles pulp
Against the silver blades which, music-smitten,
Woo on the goddess's barge, and she, pearl-sphered,
Leans forward, gold hair on curds bosom dripping
And snuffs the crinkled incense. Doves descend
And nymphs elaborately girt with swags
Draw back the pleated clouds from a blue sea
Where a plump brig pursues a spouting whale.
A crowd waits. In that beach of sunbrowned limbs
Observe the curls, wine-spattered chins, great breasts
And now we see that Loves with coloured tapes
Haul up the vessel.
              Get out, pay the fare,
  And in we go. It is a cheap hotel;
  The sheets are clean; and now they know us well.

XIII

I could inventory all the offices
That make more palatable your skeleton;
The various over-valued orifices;
The sense-receptors love is moulded on.
I know what kiss conditions what reflex
To crook the leverage by which you move.
I hate the hot condition of my sex,
And yet, like any chanticleer, I love.
Is it the act alone which I adore,
Careless of whom so the delight is mine?
No, for the act alone offends me more,
A matter for that charlatan, the spine.
    Mark me as one whom my low breeding mocks
    Loving to loathe my love's cold paradox.

XIV

My notes on love: – like an electric shock
Hated yet grasped and cannot now let go.
A wind impalpable that blows one way
All the mind's stiff and treelike qualities,
A snare of flesh in which the soul has tripped
And brought it on its face, the human way.
I am much skilled in derogation's art –
Will you hear more or answer with a kiss?
Best answer, nor indeed are you unskilled
In body's older *dialectice*
Where thesis and antithesis achieve
By friction a diviner synthesis.
   How oft have we disputed! Till the skies
   Paling, have bade us cease philosophize.

XV

When I could bite my tongue out in desire
To have your body, local now to me,
You were a woman and your proper image
Unvarying on the black screen of night,
What are you now? A thigh, a smile, an odour:
A cloud of anecdotes and fed desires
Bubblingly unfolds inside my brain
To vex its vision with a monstrous beast.
There is no pure or intellectual you
But flesh usurps the brain's forsaken throne
And soaked in vision as in native lymph
Responds convulsively to sight of you:
   Give us this day, O Lord, our daily bread.
   The hungry flesh looks up and is not fed.

XVI

Even the old Egyptians had more tact
Than you, complaining I was cold to touch
Whom winter winds had battered as I crept
Through lonely streets to sneak up draughty stairs.
Be still, be still! The natural warmth we own
Endlessly monotonously stoked
And guarded as we can from puffing death

Suffices for a while to kiss and cling
But this same hand you warmed between our breasts
Consumes the marrow of my roaring bones
And spite of all the sheets we wrapped us in
Our furnaced hearts will burn themselves to death,
   And we'll not try, we two, when we are dead
     Like ignorant ghosts, to warm ourselves in bed.

XVII

If I have loved you mainly with my brain
Until it sizzled in its pan like milk
Reproach me not; I cannot hope to prove
My genuine passion with prodigious feats
That bawds and bards might celebrate in sheets.
You know the thing I am; then how I love
Mark the outrageous froth upon my lips
And the hoarse fancies of delirium.
The brain that sways me, in no rite revered,
You have inflamed, distended, pumped with blood.
Yes, you have heard these lips botch genteel verse,
The comfortable murmur of delight
   Expect it not yourself; nor from them ask
     More than the slobber of love's prentice task.

XVIII

In Nature's factory not laggard workers
We've yet produced no trophy of our skill
And she may well dismiss us both as shirkers
Barren by no misfortune but ill-will.
Yet she approves the ruby's fruitless splendour
And wastes on hairy nostrils her perfume:
Let her, so spendthrift, be to lovers tender
And take these songs as produce of your womb;
Time will destroy them but they'll dance as long
As coloured flies or the short hopes of spring
And let her know we shall not do her wrong,
But every shift we work on, I shall sing,
   Wherefore, industrious labourer, I write
     While the days' light holds, and still work at night.

XIX

If I have shocked you that dislikes to hear
The thing named you so excellently do
Forgive me love, for I am fighting foes
    You know not, proud in your unmortgaged flesh.
The body of my song is too corrupt,
Foul with the staleness of great athletes' beds
I could not trick her out in virgin clothes
To pass as honest among worldly men,
And if I have bewhored her to the skies
Accept it not insultingly in me
That sucked fresh vigour from your tender lips
And the reviving greenness of your breasts.
    We have been honest and song's naked sight
    Now promises unpalated delight.

XX

In which we shall have earned the rose the rose
Whose petals crumpled by a thousand thighs
Were virgin and unfingered once God knows
Then worth the scented burthen of our sighs.
I have been niggard of enjoying spring
But yet the time must come when a ripe Muse
May hear the name pronounced without a grin
And automatic twitching of her hams.
Yes, even the wood's great pimp the nightingale
In the full flood of meretricious song
Set on by his unholy bawd the moon
May be permitted to observe our love
And sing of it, no more a leering foe,
As once he used, two thousand years ago.

THE ART OF DYING

(An Elegy)

Is it not time to study how to die
Against the time Death's mystery we ply
Once Life's poor chided journeyman – that state
In which we shall endure longer than Fate

And still but in the raw novitiate be
When Nature's Master writes his last decree.
When by Time's death freed from his annual cess
Full burgesses, we enter nothingness?

Old Seneca has much rehearsed his death
And finding to expel his quiet breath
Is no more pain to him than to inspire it,
Reasons to breathe life out when death require it
No worse than breathing in life with a cry,
The harsh experience of our infancy;
Suspects he was enamoured of the womb
As now of life (then feared as now the tomb)
Proposing logically once dead to hate
As much the prospect of a further state.
So revellers will outwatch the starry skies
And once recumbent are as loth to rise.

Certain it is, those who would much skilled be
In death's still unexplored philosophy
And wormy dialectic, know it best
To have some formulas to fence one's breast
Against hope's trespass; sharp dilemmas make.
Like him, wit's saint, whom death came near to break,
Whose spirit was a dirty thundercloud
Releasing poetry, to passion vowed
Then God (both incarnations of the shroud)
We ripe some comfort in the grapes which dress
Not vine, but grave-yards, make death's hard feet press
A mithradatë from his burial vats
To poison and cure too. The burning ghats
In whose smoke body imitates its breath
Will thus instruct you in the art of death,
How, public hermits, the great dead put by
The chafe of chains, the cares of liberty,
And for perdition count the world well lost,
That most care-free untrammelled thing, a ghost.
Such doctors, expert in the schools' abuse,
Twist life's pert pupil-cherubs in a noose:
If you still sport youth's clear rebellious rose
When the grave's antique scissors on you close
Reflect you have some forty gustless years
Of wambling sorrow, age's easy tears,

Scaped by this stratagem. If you are come
To bed or crutch when death inverts his thumb
Well, the fool clothes in shrouds and lets you lie
In his great hostel in your bankruptcy.
If you are humble, think that over it
Rude men will tramp, and on your ashes spit;
If you are one whom calm Philosophy
Taught men all equal, then, so here they'll be;
If you are proud, think, ere that second birth
You now would own, but then will be the earth.

Well, you are human and you have in dreams
Seen a strange blossom which no earth's gross streams
Could diet; in the corridors of sleep
You met a spirit, felt the midnight weep
Around you both, such currents did both move
As it is profanation to call Love;
You have loved unreasonably; the moon was queen
And told Rapunzel from her tower to lean
And loose her hair into the garden close:
The nightingale would chatter to the rose
Of desperate fables, hopes as old as death
Which, as their age imports, exchange for breath,
Your breath, and gladly given, but sleep fled,
And you wakened in your sordid bed.
But death is endless sleep, so when you die
With these short hopes you'll live eternally:
If this you doubt at least certain remain
This kind of thing will not vex you again,
No want perplex more the exhausted brain.

New Senecals esteem the self-pierced heart
The coarsest craftsman in the dying art
Where all things walk in shadow, fly extremes,
Reciprocate like tides and wind like streams.
They reason, since death magnet is of life
Which men avoid by constant strife,
Since fruit and water always downwards tend
And when birds rest their pinions they descend,
None should advance their death. Though life's a maze
None overlong in its labyrinth strays.
There are a million fatal figures; chance
Conspires with Time always to change the dance

And he who makes his exit ere his cue
May be reborn to act his piece anew,
Or wander restless while his fellows lie
Their good fight fought, at length allowed to die.

Deceiving looks; the angels that we paint
Are often less ethereal than a saint
Or even than a youth of vulgar clay
But then these have not such bright minds as they
Whose heart-strings are of flame, who bear within
A small piece of the heaven where they've been;
And let our poppy tell you that the rose
Has never made a corpse's eyes unclose,
That to this patron saint of living, prayers
Are useless, roses on a grave are jeers,
But let one living seek *her* aid and part
His lips, so she may throne within his heart
And in an hour or two that Roman peace
Will be established where rebellions cease.
This flower is sacred to death's anchorite
Who meditates death's office every night
And when the natural poppy of the brain
Bids him compose himself for sleep again
And up the stairs the smoky candles pass
The chamber-ritual serves as his Black Mass.
Thus goes the meditation – when I slide
Day's garments off and lay them all aside
I think that flesh which fits me like a glove
Must all be slipped off at the last remove.
Thus when I lie in bed and draw about
The flaxen webs to keep the sharp cold out
I see the day when they will wash my skin
And search for a white cloth to wrap me in
Trusting that as the angels walk in white
Their friend to such fair garments will have right;
But I'll not pray or hope my shroud will be
Fit token of my final innocency,
Old-childhood; for I hold it far from fair,
Seeing the dirty breezes man must dare,
The various rubbish that the world's winds sift,
He should quit life with an unsullied shift.
No, what I think a corpse's jacket shows
Is, bitter cold's the world to which he goes,

And that thin sheet may shield the soul at first
A little from the soil's amorous thirst
Until she's used to death's austerity
And is more practised simply not to be.

And then put out the light! Never will sleep
Come when the lights their sharp distraction keep,
Nor will your wished-for peace delight the mind
Until Life's candle gutters in the wind.
It's dark, as you'll be on your bed of death,
Waiting for peace to rule your rebel breath
And give the soul her quittance. There are those
Who feel before sleep's fingers round them close
A stifling heaviness, a mountain weight
That sits upon the snoring mind like fate:
Then think of the death-pangs you must endure
Before your peace of mind's at last secure,
Think of the weight of soil that men will heap
Upon your body lest you wake from sleep.

Murmur your childhood's prayers under your breath
But your God's name replace by that of death,
For death the greatest of salvations is
And none has proved more permanent than this.
Solomon in the end a heathen turned
But not the ficklest Christian ever burned.
Ev'n God they say his Might in flesh once cased
And with a death his deity disgraced
But that was to save man while living, plain
Enough it is that the attempt was vain.
You can still save yourself: the final doom
Of the To-morrow that must always come;
Revenge; ingratitude; remorse; hate; all
The misdemeanours that men living call.
Yes, let a score of Gods die for you, you
Can do as much, can die for yourself too
And drag perfection level with your head
(For what's perfection except to be dead,
Life's largest and unalterable sum,
Soul's last eternal equilibrium?)
Take the old road; it climbs a steady slope
To the hill's brow, then leaves the rest to hope.
The last time speaking, for the last time fed,

Start, wrap your cloak about your hoary head
And, loosening the clasping hands from round you, glide
Out into the deserted countryside.
Just for this trifling distance you must go
Companionless, a stoic heel-and-toe,
But do not fear, since millions have passed
This way (which everyone must tread at last)
Without complaint, and like the punctual host
Of heaven gleams each cold and distant ghost
Alone in the vast ether; in our sight
Some trepidations foreign to pure light
May make them shudder, but in truth all are
Content and constant as the Polar Star
There, where the sea from useless labour rests
And hangs unmoving at the heaven's breasts.

ORESTES

APOLLO

I God unveiling from the clouds my glory
Consent to wait in this consulting room
From simple habit. When the clockwork ticks,
Caught up in the machinery of verse,
I automatically descend. The sinners
No longer clasp in suppliance my bare shins
But seated on a chair (turned to the light)
Cling to the horns of an impressive desk
On which an Austrian wizard combs his beard,
Yet as I couched upon a chilly cloud
A cry of suppliance rose – or snuffle rather –
Imploring for its aid old-fashioned gods.
I rose and dressed, shot down the lift of heaven,
And here I am. The air was thick with fog;
It scarcely cleared at my terrific nod;
My hyacinthine locks are out of curl.
No matter! for the lovely groves are shorn
And the clear lustral brooks run dry, run dry
Or bear their load of sewage to the sea.
As I came in I saw a queue of suppliants;

The wizard warned me that my sacred limbs
Might rouse emotions foreign to his goal
In these distressed young females. Let it be.
I must display my fine development;
A god must keep the attributes of godhead
And if thine eye offend thee, pluck it out.
So here we are, and in this temple wait.

THE WATCHMAN

Temple he calls it. That's the best I've heard!
It's the consulting-room of Dr. Tape.

APOLLO

Who is this fellow with the prosing style?

THE WATCHMAN

I saw the boy-scouts' beacon start its run
And how its fiery message crisped and curled
Upon the broad chins of the solemn hills
Until night's razor shaved the glad news off.

APOLLO

Ah that sounds more familiar! Carry on!

THE WATCHMAN

Three thousand years ago I saw that light
And saw the sharp face of the king my lord
Caught like a mad bull in that wicked net,
Nor, though three thousand more pass, can forget.
I cannot learn the wisdom of that death
For I am dead and I forget the rest...
   Now my new thoughts march on, and almost seem
The roted speech of a dim stage-player
Whose words are what the dramatists confer.
Once I could damn straight out the gods on high
But now the gods are subject till they die
To God knows what; the wheel of living gleams
And new mutations upset old *régimes* –

APOLLO

I know! You're that old idler on the roof
Who saw the whole thing done – the crime itself!

THE WATCHMAN

– Her mind a hell she stood there at the gate
And watched her husband pass into his fate.
In hell she stands now; waits to do the deed
Of which what earthly action was the seed?
The death at Aulis? – the young girl who saw
The sober fillet of the priest with awe
Then screamed, as sharp across her tight-stretched throat
Crawled that cold edge to the kine's death devote?
Or farther back? To unaccustomed meat –

APOLLO

You may well ask! Desist my friend I pray.
You hardly know what metaphysics is,
Much less the venomed problem that you pose.
We gods are not concerned with who struck first
But who struck whom. Why do you look around?

THE WATCHMAN

Your voice, Sir, always had a special power
And now it sounds with its familiar charm
Surely it will arouse the nightingales?
Yes, here they come, dressed in their black tailcoats,
White-bowed and rubicund, with polished hair;
Fiddle to chin or baton in the hands
And, bowing to the god once, twice, begin: –

THE NIGHTINGALES

  The City is fallen! fallen!
    Dead are the bright-greaved heroes,
      Dead are the besieged, the attackers.
  Preserved in earthenware
    The ashes of high-born soldiers
      Are clasped to shadowy bosoms.
  Who tramps in the meadows of fables
    To bring back the dead to the dead?

      To those phantastic sweethearts
    Who found War a money-lender
      Extorting his cent per cent
         For every golden warrior?

  A Fury perched on this house
    Snuffling the sweat of sorrow
    And the deflowered Cassandra
  Nipped in the Python's coils
    Screamed as the knife struck inwards.
      Screamed. Ah God, we heard her!
  O cursed unhappy Atridae
    Come not this cold night seeking
      To find why you lived and suffered!
  You prisoners of Shadows!

  "Not we; dream rapes our City
    Come in array to save us."

Not enough that our lovely
  Voice, to the stars arising
    Sings while the rose is dumb?
Not that our notes are golden
  And mirrored in song's fountains
    Even pain has beauty?
No more knock at the threshold
  With boneless beating hands
    To rouse a House of Shadows.
Our song eludes the darkness
  In memory persisting.
    You like the rose are tongueless.

APOLLO

All good advice and, taken thrice a day
Would cure an obstinate ailment. Men are men
And when I was an oracle I found
That diet and hard exercise prescribed
Soon cost me fame and money. Men want more:
To cast a dagger at the frowning sky
Or fish the virgin oyster from its bed
And broil its glittering pearls in pigeon's milk.

THE WATCHMAN

It's as you please, Sir. You can call the tune.
Strike up, you fellows there, and try again.

THE NIGHTINGALES

Out of the loins of Time: earth forming; life flooding;
    mind-blowing:
        Spirted delight.
The living juice of it crusts on the thighs of the sea,
And out of sea's caverns risen, Venus, wet from the womb,
        Decks it with Night.

On the sky's base it hangs; crowns burning, flowers blooming;
    beasts barking;
        A wasps' nest of stars;
And we hear their orderly tramp as they stamp on our heads;
And the causeway of bodies works and ferments, crushed
    with the beat
        Of their hooves, of their cars.

Even the gods hear the clatter; thrones shaking; robes shredding;
    crowns bending
        They slide from the sky,
And the shepherd's staff points at these flaming comets with awe;
They have fallen before the cohorts of invisible law;
        Their hulks earth-stranded lie.

All things are born and die. Pears ripe; maids marry;
    stars drop.
        All is law's slave.
Why should we struggle or fret? Let us beat the ground
    with our feet.
Let us mate and rear children; grow beards, pass laws,
    and forget,
        Go quiet to the grave!

THE WATCHMAN

That was good stuff straight from the leader page.
I'd give a pound to have my young ones hear it.
That was the way my mother brought me up.

APOLLO

I'll make no doubt she prosed on like yourself.
You've caught the trick nodding by your coke-bucket.
Be careful or your old beard will catch fire!
But this won't do. I was a god of fashion
And never stood *démodé* devotees.
No thirsty tongues would lick this dry stuff up:
They long to slap the fat sun's rosy cheeks
Or foxtrot with a whale in Reykjavik
Where the winds howl from Arctic loneliness.

THE WATCHMAN

God bless my soul! Are you in earnest, Sir?
Well, you have heard him, friends. So do your best!

THE NIGHTINGALES

I have been unfamiliar with the best;
I have seen the sirens nodding each to each
And Aphrodite in her woollen vest
Unloose her girdle to one man alone.
I have been blown
By eager storms beneath most monstrous wrecks
While beauty puffed off the old cliffs like hair
Making a net to catch the sunset in.

Ohe! Ohe!
Entrechat quatre! Entrechat six!
Entrechat! Pirouette!
Entrechat? Tour en l'air!
So goes the measure.
So leaps my treasure.
Pas de deux! Pas de seul!
Higher and higher,
Into the fire
And burned to a cinder.

They took it and broke it and gave each to each
And every day in memory of me
Cause it to be performed at all high altars
Or every pious quorum of eleven –

We know the twelfth and how his bowels gushed out
Or else he hanged him in a potter's field,
For I forget the story
As I grew old and sere
That have the fair breasts of young women known
What time they came to seek me on tip-toe;
But now I chase them down the sordid alleys
With the blue bloodhounds baying on my heels.
It is a fond, most melancholy story
And I could sit on the damp ground all day
But reasons of hygiene forbid me this.

But I love Mamie
And she loves me.
Most kissable
Most kissable
Girl you could see!

And so they set him nodding on the stage,
A marionette of sixty who flew round
Jerked by the strings of dancing and strong drink
While all the boys and maidens gathered there
And urged him on the weary paths of sin.
Are we not poxy? Or so unrepressed
That our delivered brains have strewn the floor
And now we dance on them with printless toe?

But hist! A faun,
And after him
A score or more
Of Attic virgins,
Fair frieze enwrought
In Oxford attitudes!
Arms bent; legs prinked;
Chins back; curled wigs;
White drapery and toes.

Was it for this that Elgin Athens sacked
And the Turk hurled about great cannon balls
And Fate choked Isadora with a scarf?
These drowned sea-maidens with their weedy hair
And whelks upon the eyes are rotting ghosts
Drifting about the quiet yards of dream.

I have no love for them, no, not for one.
I count it most unpleasant to be struck
As I grope round, by a bone-slimy hand
The quintain of my unhandy way with corpses.

Let me live quietly and with care consider
Whether it was that after all I did err,
Till metamorphic autumn fire my brains
And then I settle down. Rheumatic pains
A while will give me substance for complaint
And then I pass, a poor discarded saint
Into the quietness of the famous grave
About which I much information have.

While negro fiddlers
To cheap jazz bobbing
Roll their eyes:
Thump! Thump! Thumpah!
Thump! Thump! Thumpah!
Thump! Thump! Thumpah!
Beat the ground,
Shake the hips, .
Slap the breast.
Thump! Thump! Thumpah!
Thump! Thump! Thumpah!

No matter! Peace, O maggot of the brains
And all barbaric embryos of thought
That lord it in the soft subconscious of black space.
Nigger or Mongol or what chance may bring
To the opprobrious *Homo sapiens*
Listen! we have the sick with us to-night
So let us pray.
Where that great angel of the stethoscope
Looks westward; ay, look well and puff him on
What pale prescription out of the fat shades
May hale him, messenger of manic dream.
A little while to us the keys are given
And the bronze canons of dramatic art
To blast the evil out of these bloat souls
While light persists. Let all love's sailors tossed
This night upon a stormy pillow; all
Murderers with thrawn necks and evil eyes;

All pale adulterers perverting clean beds
And every lax-bowelled dreamer torn with ruth
Pray with us;
And O ye Furies spare the hapless youth!
I have in my sheer pity writ this page
(The artist speaks)
I have observed the suffering in their eyes.
Poor children! I will chafe their frozen hands
And give them of my knowledge hardly won
By long enjoyment of my mature life
(You may rely on my entire discretion
To go off-stage when I blow out my brains).
The adventitious pity beauty brings
Shall be the cobweb clapped on this heart's cut.
Most kind, most noble honourable lords,
Of vast creation's dunghill cocks and kings,
Vouchsafe to hear our prayer, and bend your eyes
To observe a little fable, pastoral
And artless, fit for children, yet has wit.
Amen!

THE WATCHMAN

They call that singing? No, no, no, no, no!

APOLLO

Excellent! really excellent, little birds!
A God, I weep; and heavenly saline flows
At such pathetic music. Come, play on –
But soft, here is my suppliant! And late!
Why are you late? Being a god, myself
Answers the question, that a traffic block
Delayed you. And the traffic of your fear?
Ah my young friend, a wiser man than you
Remarked that care clung to one's horse's rump –
New skies the exile finds but his old soul.
   But he ignores me. Sniffs at your coke-bucket,
Ignores you too. These modern youths are blind
To the old generations of the gods
Yet still, by his sick eye and lagging tread
He hears the furies snuffling at his tail.

ORESTES

And when the doctor presses down my tongue
I shall repeat the accustomed formula –
Ar-r; and then he asks *How are our motions?*
I see...And have you any business worries?
Dr, I stabbed my mother in the breast.
Her head rolled forward. Sister held it back
And the blood dripping from her on the floor
Made a small pool. My father on all fours,
A shade but greedy, licked the fluid up
Until we basted him across the pate:
   "Be off! Papa! We've done the proper thing
By you, and you'll not fatten on her blood
To come to earth again. Shoo! both you shades
And fight it out in earth's sulphuric womb."
   Then Sister, letting go the hair, sat down
And wiped her hands. "Well, that's a dirty job
But finished. We have done our duty, dear.
God, how she squealed! A pig would be more quiet,
But mother always was so sentimental."
   I answered: "Do you hear a sort of noise?"
"A sort of noise?"
                "Yes, a kind of sniffing?"
"Orestes, have you had a drop too much?
Not that I blame you!"
                "No I've had no drink;
But I can hear a curious doglike snarling."
   Later of course they came, snake-haired, thin-dugged
And squawking, sitting on my bed all night
Or perched behind my chair with clapping wings.
I drove to Wick at 60 m.p.h.
And found them curled beneath the tonneau cover
And when I flew to Moscow on the Moth
They hung head-downwards from the fuselage.
I gave up bathing in the South of France
Seeing them crawling in the blue profound
Below me, spitting soft bubbles at my eyes.
Tape still remains: the hope of parricides
And only bulwark of incestuous love.
I will sit down and wait till he comes back.

CLYTEMNESTRA

Guess who it is, Orestes, a surprise!

ORESTES

Electra! Take your fingers off my eyes!
I thought it was the Furies. You made me jump.

CLYTEMNESTRA

Wrong! It's me!

ORESTES

Mother! But you are dead.

CLYTEMNESTRA

Yes, dead and damned, my boy; and so are you.

ORESTES

True. I forgot that I was dead and doomed.
They left me dead in Athens so long ago
And now I walk this draughty interspace,
A phantom with the easy ways of speech.

CLYTEMNESTRA

And I am doubly dead: once, killed by you:
Twice, left for dead in Athens long ago.

ORESTES

But Sophocles gave me a sweet old age...

CLYTEMNESTRA

A thing no poet upon earth can do
And those in hell have long forgotten it.
These men will give you murder, rapine, love,
But not the obscure and peaceful latter end
That you desire, and then the unknown grave.

ORESTES

And what do you want, with your still-bleeding breast?

CLYTEMNESTRA

I want my rights; I want to see you damned.

ORESTES

And will my suffering make yours the lighter?

CLYTEMNESTRA

No. But it is the essence of my being
Merely to want all Fate permits to me.
That is my ego, should I let you off
Then I should vanish like a twist of smoke.

ORESTES

It is three thousand years since the knife flashed
And you fell forwards; and I jumped back shivering.

CLYTEMNESTRA

No matter. Time is nothing.

THE WATCHMAN

                        You are right.
They'd swing him after thirty thousand years.

ORESTES

Old man, they cannot hang me for a thought.
I only killed her in a childish dream.

THE WATCHMAN

Then what the devil are you whining for?

ORESTES

Because I only did it in a dream
They cannot punish or forgive my sin.
Nor can I die; for I too am a dream.
I cannot cut my throat or lose my wits
Or swallow arsenic or found a Church.
I soothed my jangled nerves in days gone by
With bellowing thunder into Jove's vast ear
Or serenading with melodious voice

The pity-dropping balconies of Heaven.
Nowadays I can only sit and whine.

CLYTEMNESTRA

And waste our time! Apollo, Lord of song
And Arbiter of life, you know the rules!
Although this suppliant clasps your pedestal
Regard a mother's immemorial rights.

ORESTES

Let me with lustral water lave me clean!

APOLLO

Alas my friend, it's full of chemicals
And runs beneath us with the mains and gas.
The lady's right. The Furies are unpleasant
Granted. It's their *métier*. They exist;
There were no Furies until man was born,
You and your kidney have created them,
So take them as they come. And here they come.

THE WATCHMAN

God bless my soul, what unpleasant old hags.
No wonder the poor nightingales flew off.

THE FURIES

There was an old man of the Nile
Who lived in colossal style.
    But he lived so long
    His liver went wrong
And he died of a surfeit of bile.

There was an old man of Cathay
Who just lived for day after day.
    When they asked him, "Why
    Don't you do or die?"
He answered, "I like my own way."

There was a young man of the West
Whose wardrobe fell on his chest

      And rather than ask
      For help in a task
He gnawed his heart out of his breast.

We can report remarkable behaviour
Of every sainted race in every age.
We have observed in detail Christ's psychosis
And the neurotic fits of Socrates.
We've watched the obsession of each civilization
Gather in some great abscess of a city
And burst at last in pale grey floods of plague
Or the vermilion haemorrhage of war.

We have published a monograph on trophallaxis
Exhibiting the human parasite:
Its sexual habits and autophagy,
Its aberrance, self-mutilation, fits.
We are proudest of our patented man-poison
Which will not make a stench. It's guaranteed.
It is secreted in the pest's intestines.
He drinks; it swells; he crawls away and dies

Or gouges out his gaster with his nails
If he belongs to the neurotic whites.
And God himself has signed a testimonial
To its effect in Europe's happy home
Which was infested with the lesser Nordic.
A minute application was enough:
They dashed out to the nearest open space
To beat and bung each other for four years.

God recommends another application
But we incline far more to *laissez-faire*.
There is a wandering mania in the eyes
That shows us the survivors are diseased.
Yes, we submit, this slow degeneration
With their sterility, will do the trick.
Then we can settle with the yellow species
And the more vigorous and larger black.

Orestes has a certain native toughness.
He knows his science, poetry, and Freud;
He has his dreams of economic bliss;

He cleans his teeth; his conscience; and his bowels.
But we shall get him for his brain breeds worms.
Its very warmth and vigour will destroy him.
He'd be O.K. if had had no parents
And could restrain from eating tasteful food
Or the sly bliss of talk or reproduction
But as it is, we fear that he must go.

Three thousand years upon the plank of death
He's tottered dangerously but kept his grip;
Now he's unsafer than he ever was
Because he's seen at last what lies below him.
Christ told him God had hung a net down there;
Muhammed mentioned magnets in his toes;
Huxley suggested gravity was with him;
But now he knows one slip will break his neck.

Each night I have descended into hell
Which is like Brighton on a larger scale.
I found the passionate heat intolerable
But this resort is famous for its sun.

I have been that disgusting androgyne
Which every human soul bears in its breast
And wandering in the meadows of perversion
Was shocked to meet a Bishop and a dean,
Professors, and two Secretaries of State.
The Devil waits for all of us in dream
And our Orestes hardly dares to sleep.
He knows the dangers of that haunted deep
Where the full-bosomed Mermaid twangs her harp
Strung with the horny guts of mariners:

> "Down, down!
> Come away, come away
> Children dear!
> Don't be afraid,
> Here you may hate
> Father or mother,
> Kill your brother.
> Spit on this one;
> Wound the other.
> Down in my dark,

> Down in my cosy,
> Down in my breast!
> Come away, come away,
> Children dear!
> All for your pleasure,
> All for delight,
> Wishing is dreaming,
> Dreaming is having,
> Having dreaming,
> Dreaming die!"

And the gnarled lunatics with broadnailed paws
Will dig you out of consecrated ground
And shear your flesh to shreds in snuffling glee.

Yes, though your brain be bladder-tight with wit
Your soles are leaden, and they'll drag you down,
Ten fathoms down, into the dark profound
And here upset you. Up you go again
Feet first and bobbing, and so bobbing starve.

I have seen angels in their lutany
Chaunting their poems to God's backward parts
And the great glory thereof scorched mine eyes.
And you, Orestes, if you ply the scourge
And bant and sterilize and hate the flesh
May yet attain to the obsequious angels
But maybe not. Discuss it with the worms.
You may get through to Heaven with your trunk
Or two worm-nibbled ankles may skip through
Puzzling St. Peter, Heaven's Musick-master,
What Heaven-praising instrument you'll play.

I have been loving to my fellow men
Humiliating them with charity
I hope; until they knew their proper place
And let me stroke their heads with my wet palm.
I have died for them; greater love hath none
Than this; which they declared *Felo de se.*
I have been hopeful, and in phantasy
Have flushed the gilded butterflies of dream;
They jailed me as drunk and disorderly.
So be it. Three months in Leviathan

And tabled at his kidney, I endured,
The mystic hero of our human race,
Then hacked my way out, left the beast for dead,
And stepped on shore, fishy and deified,
Snuffing up the thick incense as my due
Until they crucified me for a myth.

We have had orgies
And mixed our limbs round the warm fumes of wine
But the lights guttered and Brown started up
In the cold embrace of paralysis.

I ripped the liver from a mighty man
And pouched it as a talisman; it swung
At my hips lightly; but as the weeks passed
Grew heavier and heavier. Now it weighs me down
And this giant burden tugging at my loins
Will stretch me on my tracks to starve to death
Or be ate up by the marauding wolves.

Surely to die were best! And some say, Yes;
But others, No and recommend the clouds
Where wind blows not, and no rain falls they say
But we are dieted with the god's food
And fly light-heeled – and he in demonstration
Outstretches arms, leaps, falls, and is caught up
By the attentive warder, who lugs him off
To a new course of padded cell and purge.

Shall we then join the company of ants,
Each pushing a peanut onward with his nose
Among the glorious servitors of Mansoul?
The nest comes first; the nest must be preserved;
The nest is warm and has a sacred smell.
Long live the nest and every antish instinct!
Till the broad buttocks of Almighty God
Placed on the nest, squash us, brood, workers, queen.
(Some of us, sly-eyed cynical old ants
Bite the God's hams, and make him ouch with pain
Or at least air our views below our breaths
Which wiser ants condemn and as the juice
Spurts from their abdomens, bless Him Who sits.)

Thus the world wags; and every night to hell
Where your sincerest wish is gratified
(And so is hell) and every morn to earth
Gladly return, and every night to hell
As glad go back, Orestes! and like hounds
We snuffle at your heels to keep you spry
Until you cough blood, fall between two stools
And fly apart in some preposterous mania,
Torn by the rival claims of nonsense dreams
Which none on earth can satisfy at once.

APOLLO

May I felicitate you, my dear ladies?
I'm dumbfounded by your modernity.

ORESTES

Supposing I stand up to you, you hags
And you too, Mother! Knowing you are dreams,
Offer my cheeks to your infernal nails
And say: "Go, do your worst. You are pure shades
Without a vote or household! You are dreams
And if you frighten me I shall awake!"?

APOLLO

You can of course do that.

THE FURIES

He can't!

CLYTEMNESTRA

He daren't

APOLLO

He can. But if he dare, then you and I
And this prim fabric of reflective art
Will at once crumble into dusty words.

ORESTES

And I?

APOLLO

And you'll be less. A fag-end thrown
Contemptuously upon earth's foul floor
Whom God's angelic chars disdain to salve.

THE FURIES

He pales!

CLYTEMNESTRA

He'd see me dead but not himself!

THE FURIES

(*Semi-Chorus I*)

We've got him. He's afraid of suicide.

(*Semi-Chorus II*)

Liven him with a whiff of poison gas!

(*Semi-Chorus I*)

Stir the mixture
Boil and bake;
Triturate!
Masticate!
Pound and filter
For his sake!

(*Semi-Chorus II*)

Many a long-haired parasite
In its pale and fungoid sleep,
Many a witch-faced eyeless monster
Trawl-delivered from the deep.

(*Semi-Chorus I*)

Stir a wounded pastry godling
And a harlot's leprous sap
In a cupful of dementia
From the spine's diseased tap.

(*Semi-Chorus II*)

A pinch of scurf, a cancer cell,
An old physogastrous ant.
Shake up the lickerish concoction
And ye humorous ghosts, avaunt!

Chorus

Seven times we turn about
Obedient to Planck's equation.
Nature's secrets he may touch
Now; but not salvation.

ORESTES

Yes, I'll endure. In hell, but I'll endure.
No doubt some residue of tougher salts
Will last the flames out. In the cold earth's autumn
Ripeness, with promise of increase, may come
And touch these chalky joints with hope. Survive
Orestes, with the extent of certitude
That satisfies the agriculturist
Or the bleak wizard, waiting until rain
Anatomizes the fat body, bares
The white and knobbled chassis of the flesh.

THE FURIES

You flatter yourself, boy! How can you boast
Of your decision to go on with life?
It's no decision. Here in black and white
The stage directions state you go on living
As the script requires, so you perform.

ORESTES

I do not claim the merit but the fact –
That I endure, that I attain at last
What profit to endurance may accrue.

APOLLO

Well, I for one cannot endure this place
And I must go. Already on my skin
These human sorrows crust in rancid sweat

Requiring the cool hands of flower-fed nymphs
Smudged with ambrosia, to ease me of it.

   I think I am a reasonable god
And therefore I suggest a compromise.
You, young Orestes, make a sacrifice
To the maternal *manes*, and what else
My priest requires in ritual – and pay.
You, Clytemnestra, drop your present *rôle*
And play the tame perhaps but restful part
Of martyred and forgiving wife and mother
(No questions asked of Agamemnon's death).
And you, dear ladies, shall receive a church
Or theatre or chair in this fair prospect
Where the Thames gushes on the tuneful mud
And by the glittering tramlines lamp-posts rise
Spreading their pale corollas of slow light
And many a wireless set, its small mate wooing
Sings ardent, while at evening's downfall comes
Night, like a heaven-kissing cloud to bless
The peering cheeks with multi-coloured sheen
Of signs or signals; and hot water flows
Constant, the generous dower of the gods

     So morn returns; but not to me return
These songs and flashings, for the cold of heights
Enfolds me, borne afar upon the clouds
In the wing-boastful company of gulls
Sucking vain winds; while to your palates come
Daily roast offerings; fruits to please your eyes;
Flowers in profusion; Ocean's showers of fish;
Blue halls of high-piled meat; and diamonds
As gross as those with which the Tatar Khans
Pelt slaves in anger; and eternal gold
Sleeping in the old caves of Parliament,
Tun after tun, drowsier than the plump girths
Tapped cautiously by fabulous Beefeaters
Chumbling the scarlet livery of age –

          CLYTEMNESTRA

Urged by my proper malice, I refuse.

THE FURIES

And we refuse, for naught our palates pleases
But the tart odour of Orestes's sweat
Caught in the cold-lipped engine of his fear.

APOLLO

Then I ascend; and leave you to your taste.

CLYTEMNESTRA

Then I descend; and leave you to your task.

THE WATCHMAN

And I go out; and leave you for a drink.

ORESTES

And so you have me! Let me see your worst!
What puppet shows with bang-pate skeletons
And red-nosed revenants hiccupping curses?

THE FURIES

We have few properties. Here is our worst.

ORESTES

A mirror! Very unpleasant I admit.
I have a morning-afterish aspect.
Is this a symbol?

THE FURIES

        No, a gentle hint.
And now good-bye. We need not hang around you
Now that you are alone. We have no secrets
But when you've company, hearing the cars
And voices, we slide down the bannisters
And grimace at the guests.

ORESTES

        Infant terrors!

THE FURIES

Something of the sort. But now the party's over
Leaving you alone among the bits
We sneak upstairs again and into bed –
Not but that later, in the chilly morn
You may not hear us chuckling in the attic
And speculate what tricks you will discover
When you get up – perhaps a headless cat
Or an under-footman with his eyes gouged out.

ORESTES

You're right. I see we understand each other well.

THE FURIES

Too well! And if you'll unbutton your waistcoat
Into your breast we'll vanish like a smoke.

ORESTES

There's something quite maternal in the gesture...

THE FURIES

And rightly! Dieting at your hairy bosom
We've hung like bats, swelling and dropping off
With muffled thuds, sharp-tempered from sour wind
Or knelt and made our trustful orisons:
"Blessed be the brain that bore us and the complex
That gave us suck!"

ORESTES

     Here, changelings! Ah, they've gone.
And I'm alone, while at my ankle hangs
The scabbed and rusty world to chafe my steps.
God helped my grandpapa whose birth-stained clothes
Were whitened in the laundry of the Church
But no push-button God will bleach for me
The crime I never did except in sleep.
I am guilty of that resortful city
Which rose to stately music from a sea
Of rippling flesh, splashed by divine saliva
And full of snub-nosed ministers of pleasure

Holding out hot right hands in amity;
Its tower of ivory on the low hills watching,
Where my young princess, turning in her sleep,
Blinked to affright the itch-foot butterfly
Whose colour yet well pleased her. Roses fall
From the black lunar space above in torrents
And whales, rolling idly in the thick perfume,
Chased by the shallow boats of fair-haired gods,
Tail-tossed them skywards like young meteors.
Here in the contemplative knowing air
I fly and guide, stroking the tinkling stars
To teach them geometry from my school books,
Strange books, old books, that give me equal power
To any calm-eyed and long-bearded wizard.
Here like a pulsing fountain Nightingale
Jets his gold music, in strong rhythmic floods.

Marble the city is and in the lake
An image hangs unmoving at its breast,
Image but lovelier, which to its own bosom
Imparts a bright reflection lovelier still;
Yet crime; all crime. The niggling decalogue
Of this outrageous and harsh blue-chinned world
Has sent its gross-booted detectives here
To pluck the sheets away and, thus exposed
To law's cold winds and words' corruptive spray
The rocket-slender turrets of the city
Have crumbled, fell on me and beat
Me with the cold resentful hands of bricks,
So I am bruised and broken and alone,
The Universe's delinquent, condemned
To jeers and uncompanionable vermin.

ELECTRA

You do sound sorry for yourself, old chap!

ORESTES

Thank God you've come, Electra! I've been mad!
The Furies –

ELECTRA

        Why do you let them rattle you?
I never care what people say to me.
Poor father! But we did the proper thing
And he can rest in peace. And so can we.

ORESTES

I know, I know. It isn't really that.
I often ask myself, What does it matter
Murdered or not, mother or anyone?
And yet that's worse, for in the final push
There's nothing matters much, not even life
Which is as well, for if we half-believed
The agonies in which the days curl up
And burn, the constant sounds of suffering flesh,
We'd bang our skulls to pieces in despair.
But is it a put-up job? and in their earths
Do foxes, Christs, and hopeless criminals
Laugh, their cups clinking, how they fooled the world?

ELECTRA

There you see, when once you think it out
You needn't worry as I always said;
It's only liver or else indigestion.
If only you would fall for some nice girl!
But not too clever, that was father's ruin,
Cassandra with her knowing airs the bitch!
I've felt so happy since I've been engaged
And he's a dear: tall and as rich as father.
His people have been sweet, for since the trial
Though we got off, the papers made such fuss
The county aren't too keen on the Atridae.

ORESTES

Lucky for you you're so insensitive!

ELECTRA

Call it that if you like. I just don't care.
I say though, who's that standing in the corner?
I didn't notice him when I came in.

ORESTES

It looks to me like father.

AGAMEMNON

Yes, it is.

ELECTRA

Father! but you're dead.

AGAMEMNON

Yes, my girl, I'm dead.
You can't find anything deader than me.

ELECTRA

Then what are you doing here?

AGAMEMNON

You should know that
For I am you – the loose skin of your sorrow
Stuffed with your love. In hell I heard your call
And I was packed in flesh. They slammed the lid
And here I am.

ELECTRA

What is it like down there?

AGAMEMNON

Dreadful, Electra! You have no idea!
We float like water-lilies on the mud
Crammed grossly millions thick in death's black swamp,
Diseased and pale of flesh. The trampling sounds
Above us. How the battle does, if well
Or ill, we know not. Yet it was our fight
And we once fed the guns whose monstrous sighs
Now shake our leaves, and round the walls of Troy
We mined and countermined. The long years through
We rot and whisper, scandalize the living
And boast, and still though dead we grow
Higher and higher rankly like the hair
Which as you know sprouts on a corpse's chin.

ELECTRA

What can I do for you?

AGAMEMNON

      Nothing but grieve.
The salt tears soaking through our slimy ceiling
Do not appease us but a shade who lacks them
Is much humiliated and despised.

ELECTRA

Then I shall mourn for ever.

AGAMEMNON

      That's my child!
And wear black clothes and keep my tombstone clean!
Never forget your poor old father, dear.
Think of his cold bones in the swamp of death
Contemptuously mumbled by the rats.

ELECTRA

Never will I forget: never – Oh my God –

ORESTES

Electra, don't break down like that. Good Lord
We all must die. It doesn't worry me.
Let the dead rest in peace and us in peace.
They're dead and done with, and our job remains
How best support and use the boring years
Of necessary life, their horrors,
Their various duties and absurd seductions.

AGAMEMNON

How dare you speak of your old father thus, Sir!
Is this your modern talk, eh? I'm to rot
Unmourned for, perhaps thrown to the dogs even?
If not your father, at least respect old age.

ORESTES

I shall grow older than you probably
Before I die, and as for being my father
You're dead, you know, and have no legal status.

ELECTRA

I cannot bear the thought that those I love
Must die and moulder; all of them must die,
The man I love, the child I hope to bear.
I want the world safe for them like a bright toy.
If they must die, I want the whole world shaken
That it dare go on calmly while they rot.

ORESTES

Oh damn our family! Can't I comfort you
If you fear death, by pointing out that life
Is so disgusting, death is a release?

ELECTRA

You can't. I know it's wrong for I love life
And my heart hurts to think of all the dead
Lying there buried in the earth like stones.

AGAMEMNON

That's right my child! But now my time is up.
As I collapse, the blood with which you filled me
Will spurt upon the floor and shades will come,
My bedfellows, to snatch a brief existence
By paddling their frail ankles in the physic.
Goodbye, my child. Remember! *sans* relief
Eternal mourning and no truce with death!

THE SHADES

Can't you hear us calling
    Child of life?
Isn't there a creepy-crawling
Memory, a dream appalling
    Of a knife.

And the painless operation
    (Safe, they said)
Then the spluttering suffocation,
The weak heart's capitulation
    To the dead?

Isn't there a mathematic
    Of despair –
Life's expectation, the emphatic
Answer of insurance, static
    Deaf to prayer?

Didn't Jones go, didn't Brown go,
    Friends of yours?
Aren't you liverish? – that tomato
Face, blood-pressure, vertigo,
    Failing powers!

Can't you hear us calling
    Little friends?
Life's a rope and we are hauling
All of you despite your squalling
    To your ends.

You lived, you see, upon our money,
    Sons of ours,
Our capital; you thought it funny
Little bees, to suck the honey
    From us flowers.

But we oppressed proletariat
    Rise at last.
We ask, and whirl death's crippling lariat,
"What do you owe the commissariat
    Of the past?"

Can't you hear us scheming
    Children dear?
How to meet you when you're dreaming,
See you, kiss you, wake you screaming:
    "I am here!"

Now we're dead you wear our breeches,
    Use our bed,
Ride our mares and hunt our bitches,
Soil the name and spend the riches
    Of the dead.

Can't you feel a nervous quiver
    In the knee?
Or a burden on the liver?
Does your scalp begin to shiver?
    It is we!

You inherited our sickness
    With the rest.
It will damn your young eyes' quickness
And you'll feel the gathering thickness
    In your breast.

Don't think we shall bear you malice
    When you come.
There's no snobbery of palace,
Shame of birth or pride of phallus
    In the tomb.

Here we lie and here we moulder
    Down at heel,
Packed like sardines breast to shoulder,
Whores in finery and the soldier
    Complete steel.

Here we wait the resurrection,
    So they say.
We shall be a queer collection
Needing sorting and dissection
    On the Day.

Never mind. It doesn't matter
    To the dead.
We shall be too bored to chatter
When we hear the struck stars patter
    Overhead.

You needn't really mind our joking.
    Just a nip.
Though your pleasure is provoking
You won't wake to find you're choking
    In our grip.

For when one's dead one's hate is powerless
    Like one's lust.
Hope's absurd. One's time is hourless
One's good intentions thrust up flowerless
    From the dust.

Can't you hear us calling
    Child! Ahoy!
In the sunlight shadows falling,
In the darkness parents bawling,
    Sunny Boy?

ELECTRA

Stop, stop! I cannot stand that ghastly noise
Of the dead crooning like a gramophone.
Always in dream they used to come to me
With something tragic in their anguish. These –
Have you no dignity in your despair?

THE SHADES

What, Miss? You watch us die! Our glazed eyes popping
And fingers scrabbling while we gobble breath.
See our dead faces like preposterous clowns
Purple and staring and the dignified
Finish in which our fleshly garb is stripped
By earth's rank humours and the faceless worms!

ORESTES

I recognize your voices! You're not shades.
You are the Furies come back to torment us.

THE SHADES

Furies or phantoms, it is all the same.
Your fathers or your conscience or your Gods
Or your heredity, we are the same
Disgusting flies from ancient sinews bred.

ORESTES

And you that made the same mistake as we
Have you no comfort equal to our hopes?
Can you not show us progress or delight?

THE SHADES

Not us wise shades! Like you we dreamed those dreams
And bit the dust. We're dead. It's the past's job
Always to herd your sort down the same cliffs
To the detested sea; and boulders roll
And whips we use, poor swine! We lack the art
To lead you on with sweet discourse of pipes.
But it is open to you, if you wish
To look up to the boughs and hear –

THE NIGHTINGALES

Sit down. The grey-flanked evening
   Browses. In the meadows
      The kine look for the herdsman
And to the field of heaven
   The cattle of the gods
      Are led by Hesperus.
Many a schooner heels
   Puffed by the grateful wind
      That runs it into harbour;
Many a worker pauses,
   Puts by his ledger, climbs
      Down from his stool and homeward.
Rest and the pleasant voices
   Of comrades flower round us.
      It is time for drinking;
And in the dusty parks
   We lie among the papers
      And kiss, or rolling back
Look up to see the radiance
   Of the eternal stars
      And the advertisements.
Soon winter comes, the snow
   Like angels' tears of pity
      Cold and superfluous
Falling, a sheet of splendour
   Yet at the touch of traffic
      Dissolving into slime.
Go, if you will and play,
   Or talk to an equal friend
      Or sit in the deepening twilight
And hear our music tell

The agonies of Gods
   Or quiet loves of mortals.

ORESTES

Nice birds! But look, they've gone.

THE SHADES

                             Of course they've gone.
We scared them. Do you think we should wait round
Forever, while you stood there, pink snout dribbling
Hoof lifted, wrapped in piggy ecstasy?
Come, you've had your stand-easy, swine. Move on!

ORESTES

And if I won't be driven? Squat plump down
In spite of all your stones and shouts to budge me?

THE SHADES

Some beasts do! Earth is littered with their bones
And if men like to, let them, we don't care.
For there are other pigs – pr'aps better pork.
But while you'll march we'll stick to you.

ORESTES

                             And we
Shall suffer always.... Is there no escape?
Must I for ever stand here cap in hand
And see poor virtue forced and hope a joke
And set my hand to warfare?

THE SHADES

                         Don't ask us.
Ask the all-blessed comfortable Gods.
The Gods may hear you if the Gods exist
And if they hear may tell you, if they know.

ORESTES

Then let us ask. Electra, lift your hands
To the all-blessed comfortable gods
As we were wont to do at mother's knee.

ELECTRA

Yes, I remember. Then we were but babes.
Later though mother used the self-same gesture
Kneeling to us. But we held the knife firm.

THE SHADES

(A touching trick learned from Euripides!)

ELECTRA

And look! In the machine descending
A deity! She shakes her thunderous aegis
And knits her virgin brow. It's our own goddess
Athene, daughter of Zeus and Wisdom's patron.

THE SHADES

I fear your eyesight's going. It's no goddess
It's only Tape returning. His doctor's hood
You call his aegis, trimmed with rabbit fur.

ORESTES

Now he comes nearer I will swear it's neither
But mother's paramour, the man Aegisthos.

ATHENE

All three are right. For as you know the gods
May shape themselves as men or beasts or women
And though no myth recounts my avatar
Yet I, Athene, was your mother's lover
Sampling with caution the delights of passion
And taking care never to get involved
Till finally, bored by love's tedium
Went and got killed or something, I forget.

These modern days the Gods must earn their bread.
Zeus as you know supports the toppling throne,
Without him the poor Empire would collapse
And Communists would rape our duchesses.
Venus at Hollywood doles out to stars
Their sex-appeal. Apollo, Lord of Jazz,
Sets our hams twitching, and I, Queen of Science,

Look after armaments and moral health
That philosophic savant, Dr. Tape.

But as for you, you shades or Furies, go!
You're merely inhibited tendencies
And now I've analysed you, quick, avaunt!
You see? They've gone. Do what you want to do.
The God works in you then, and up and on
The Vital Force will press you. We evolve
To higher things and higher. God never is
Nor was but always will be. Alexander
Explains it. I can't stop to quote at length
But you must understand that values
Are all conserved and every good you do
Lives on. Evil of course is necessary
So shut your eyes and swallow like a pill.
Each day we learn some more. New tricks, new trades
Despite Bergsonians, those Judases
We shall march on hope-flushed with rolling drums.
Now when you're dead, you're dead. The good you did
Lives after you. If you ask more of life
You're greedy.
          But, Electra, where are you going?
Without answering me she rushes out!
A goddess I foresee her end. The type
Hysteric with a bad Electra complex!
There! as I guessed, she's run straight to the Thames
And in she goes! A while her gold head bobs
What time she sings some dubious shepherd song
Buoyed by her garments. Round her neck depend
Dahlias and orchids wreathed. But now she sinks
Twice, then for ever. Drowns. Police come. Too late!

Orestes stays, being more curious.
Sit down, Orestes, or I'll lose my thread
If you keep hopping up and down. There's nothing
To worry about. You have your growing pains
Natural in adolescence. Never mind,
You will feel better when you are a man.
Meanwhile don't crush your instincts, whether sex
Or fear. But of course if you must you must.
We don't ask you to do anything wrong.
Not that we mind but it recoils on you.

God bless my soul, he's gone! A hopeless fellow.
Undoubtedly a paranoid or worse.
There he goes rushing madly through the traffic
And now he's down. The tank he's fallen against
Glides over him impassive. Now he's dead.
The Furies were in ambush. Rank bad taste
And dead against the rules. But they're no sportsmen.

Well, I had quite a lot more still to say
But it seems pointless to an empty house.
So I ascend, the tragedy resolved
By timely intervention of my godhead.

NOTES

In these *Notes* the numbers shown in brackets indicate the number of a manuscript as recorded in the list given in Alan Munton and Alan Young, *Seven Writers of the English Left: A Bibliography of Literature and Politics, 1916-1980*, New York, Garland Publishing Inc., 1981, pp.266-268.

Early Poems

Most of the poems in this section are taken from an unpublished collection in typescript which was to have been called *The Assignation and other poems*. This collection is currently in the possession of Christopher Sprigg's sister, Rosemary. Also in her possession are autograph fair copy versions of the *Smoke and Diamond* sequence and the drafts of several stages in the development of the *November the Eleventh* sequence.

The first seven poems in this section come from an autograph manuscript notebook (8.252) now in the collection of the Humanities Research Center, The University of Texas at Austin. The Humanities Research Center has other typed versions of both the *November the Eleventh* (8.255 – 8.256) and the *Smoke and Diamond* (8.261) sequences.

Four of the poems in this section – "On 'A Public School Anthology'", "On a Dead Cat", "In the Aegean", and "On Dryden" – were published previously in Paul Beard's edition of Christopher Caudwell's *Poems* (1939).

Christopher Sprigg added the original date of composition to most of the poems in the *Smoke and Diamond* sequence, as follows: "The Pursuit" 19/10/26; "Impregnable" 29/11/26; "Reason" 6/7/26; "The Double" 26/6/26; "The Song of Songs" 19/10/26; "The Chase" 19/10/26; "The Answer" 11/7/26; "The Physician" 1/10/26; "The Road" 5/9/26; "Courage" 3/11/26; "The Search" 25/11/26; "Matter" 23/11/26; "Complexity" 22/10/26; "The Device" 14/6/26; "Smoke and Diamond" 11/12/26; "More Proverbs" 9/10/26.

Point of Departure

Many of the poems in this section were collected together ready for publication by Christopher Sprigg himself. The typescript of this planned collection is now in the collection of the Humanities

Research Center, The University of Texas at Austin. The Center also holds typescripts of "Polar Expedition" (8.262) and "Heil Baldwin!" (8.263) though, again, other versions of these poems – including an autograph manuscript of "Polar Expedition" – are in the possession of Rosemary Sprigg.

The poem "High on a bough" came second in a poetry competition organised by *The Saturday Review* in 1929. It was published in *The Saturday Review* on 4 May 1929, p.610. Christopher Sprigg used the pseudonym "Albert" for his competition entry. The poem "The Ecstasy" (p.87) was originally published with the title "Once I Did Think" in *Dial* LXXXII, 3 March 1929, p.187. "Heil Baldwin!" (pp.99-115) follows closely a Communist version of the Nazi rise to power in Germany. There are numerous references to persons and events of the period, too many to list here.

A.J.P. Taylor's masterly summary of this background which forms his Introduction (pp.9-16) to Fritz Tobias *The Reichstag Fire: Legend and Truth*, Secker and Warburg, 1963 is highly recommended to anybody wishing to understand the historical background to "Heil Baldwin!". Equally highly recommended is Tobias's book which re-interprets the Reichstag fire and the subsequent trial, events which figure prominently in the poem.

Poems

All of the poems in this section are arranged as they were by Paul Beard in his edition of *Poems* by Christopher Caudwell (1939). The only omissions are the four "juvenilia" which have been transferred to the first section (Early Poems).